Living in Colonial America

Titles in the Series Include:

Living in Colonial America

EXPLORING
CULTURAL
HISTORY

Michael C. Ryan, *Book Editor*

Bruce Glassman, *Vice President*
Bonnie Szumski, *Publisher*
Helen Cothran, *Managing Editor*

GREENHAVEN
PRESS®

THOMSON
━━━━━✦━━━━━ ™
GALE

San Diego • Detroit • New York • San Francisco • Cleveland
New Haven, Conn. • Waterville, Maine • London • Munich

THOMSON
———✳———™
GALE

LIBRARY OF CONGRESS CATALOGING-IN-PUBLICATION DATA

Living in colonial America / Michael C. Ryan, book editor.
    p. cm. — (Exploring cultural history)
    Includes bibliographical references and index.
    ISBN 0-7377-1729-7 (lib. : alk. paper)
    1. United States—Social life and customs—To 1775—Sources. 2. United States—Social conditions—To 1865—Sources. 3. United States—Social life and customs—To 1775. I. Ryan, Michael C. II. Series.
    E162.L58 2004
    973.2—dc22   2003056848

Contents

Chapter 2: Religion and Education in the Colonies

Chapter 3: Colonial Entertainment

theater was important in promoting art and culture in the new land.

Foreword

Too often, history books and teachers place an overemphasis on events and dates. Students learn that key births, battles, revolutions, coronations, and assassinations occurred in certain years. But when many centuries separate these happenings from the modern world, they can seem distant, disconnected, even irrelevant.

The reality is that today's society is *not* disconnected from the societies that preceded it. In fact, modern culture is a sort of melting pot of various aspects of life in past cultures. Over the course of centuries and millennia, one culture passed on some of its traditions, in the form of customs, habits, ideas, and beliefs, to another, which modified and built on them to fit its own needs. That culture then passed on its own version of the traditions to later cultures, including today's. Pieces of everyday life in past cultures survive in our own lives, therefore. And it is often these morsels of tradition, these survivals of tried and true past experience, that people most cherish, take comfort in, and look to for guidance. As the great English scholar and archaeologist Sir Leonard Woolley put it, "We cannot divorce ourselves from our past. We are always conscious of precedents . . . and we let experience shape our views and actions."

Thus, for example, Americans and the inhabitants of a number of other modern nations can pride themselves on living by the rule of law, educating their children in formal schools, expressing themselves in literature and art, and following the moral precepts of various religions and philosophies. Yet modern society did not invent the laws, schools, literature, art, religions, and philosophies that pervade it; rather, it inherited these things from previous cultures. "Time, the great destroyer, is also the great preserver," the late, noted thinker Herbert J. Muller once observed. "It has preserved . . . the immense accumulation of products, skills, styles, customs, institutions, and ideas that make the man on the American street indebted to all the peoples of history, including some who never saw a street." In this way, ancient Mesopotamia gave the world its first cities and literature; ancient Egypt, large-scale architecture; ancient Israel, the formative concepts of Judaism,

Christianity, and Islam; ancient Greece, democracy, the theater, Olympic sports, and magnificent ceramics; ancient China, gunpowder and exotic fabrics; ancient Rome and medieval England, their pioneering legal systems; Renaissance Italy, great painting and sculpture; Elizabethan England, the birth of modern drama; and colonial America, the formative environments of the founders of the United States, the most powerful and prosperous nation in world history. Only by looking back on those peoples and how they lived can modern society understand its roots.

Not all the products of cultural history have been so constructive, however. Most ancient Greeks severely restricted the civil rights and daily lives of women, for instance; the Romans kept and abused large numbers of slaves, as did many Americans in the years preceding the Civil War; and Nazi Germany and the Soviet Union curbed or suppressed freedom of speech, assembly, and religion. Examining these negative aspects of life in various past cultures helps to expose the origins of many of the social problems that exist today; it also reminds us of the ever-present potential for people to make mistakes and pursue misguided or destructive social and economic policies.

The books in the Greenhaven Press Exploring Cultural History series provide readers with the major highlights of life in human cultures from ancient times to the present. The family, home life, food and drink, women's duties and rights, childhood and education, arts and leisure, literacy and literature, roads and means of communications, slavery, religious beliefs, and more are examined in essays grouped by theme. The essays in each volume have been chosen for their readability and edited to manageable lengths. Many are primary sources. These original voices from a past culture echo through the corridors of time and give the volume a strong feeling of immediacy and authenticity. The other essays are by historians and other modern scholars who specialize in the culture in question. An annotated table of contents, chronology, and extensive bibliography broken down by theme add clarity and context. Thus, each volume in the Greenhaven Press Exploring Cultural History series opens a unique window through which readers can gaze into a distant time and place and eavesdrop on life in a long vanished culture.

Introduction: The Colonial Landscape: Wilderness Adventures in the New World

The American frontier landscape symbolized many things to the American colonists. It represented freedom and newness, a place of unbounded material wealth and plenty. The landscape captivated the European imagination; it possessed an awe-inspiring, transcendent quality that fueled a spirit of adventure and helped to form the image of the mythic American frontiersman. The many explorers who traveled and mapped the colonial landscape illustrate these idealized notions and expectations in their journals, identifying the land as a formative characteristic of the North American colonial experience.

From the time of the "discovery," of North America, it has been envisioned in idealized terms. After stumbling upon this new continent, Christopher Columbus's initial reactions to America in 1492 reveal his vision of the land as a place of unending natural riches awaiting European exploitation. Of course, Columbus was searching for a new trade route to the Indies when he chanced upon America, and he is quick to point out that his finding is rich in resources, stating that "these lands are the most fertile, and temperate and flat and good in the whole world."[1] This indicates that the New World was important for its bountiful agricultural capabilities and its variety of flora and fauna, which could be converted into raw materials to be bought and sold in the European marketplace. This depiction and expectation of Columbus's sets the tone for centuries of idealized representations of colonial North America.

His *Log-Book* describes the landscape in paradisal terms, another common trope in writings about the colonial terrain. In it, he describes the overwhelming immensity and density of the untrammeled wilderness and celebrates the freshness of the landscape, asserting that "everything on all these coasts is so green and lovely that I do not know where to go first, and my eyes never weary of looking on this fine vegetation, which is so different from that of our own lands."[2]

As Columbus's history and ambitions indicate, the spirit of adventure and discovery encouraged many explorers to seek out the new continent. The colonial frontier provided uncharted territory for men to test their mettle, make a name for themselves, and profit from the seemingly endless wilderness. Many adventurers and traders followed Columbus, seeking the freedoms and opportunities that the European landscape did not present. Samuel de Champlain, a French trapper and trader, is a well-known early North American frontiersman. Having an intimate knowledge of the land and its inhabitants, Champlain compiled the first detailed map of the New England coast fifteen years before the arrival of the Pilgrims; he also recorded many of his explorations in and tribulations with the wilderness in journals for posterity. His life and writings reflect the romanticized vision of the American continent as a masculine testing ground, filled with wild creatures waiting to be conquered and tamed. Like Columbus, Champlain finds the feral lands he inhabits to be diverse, full of natural wonder, and offering great monetary rewards:

> There are many pretty islands here, low, and containing very fine woods and meadows, with abundance of fowl and such animals of the chase as stags, fallow-deer, roe-bucks, bears, and others, which go from the mainland to these islands. We captured a large number of these animals. There are also many beavers, not only in this river, but also in numerous other little ones that flow into it.[3]

It is evident that Champlain sees the land and its inhabitants as his for the taking. The image that he embodies—that of the self-reliant, tough, and individualistic frontiersman—exerts a profound influence on the North American consciousness and how men define themselves within the culture. Driven in part by economic motives (the fur trade) and in part by a love of the land, Champlain and his writings support the notion that life on the colonial frontier created rugged, hardy men in control of their own destinies. As novelist and writer Wallace Stegner describes them: "Dependent on their own strength and ingenuity in a strange land, they learned to dismiss tradition and old habit."[4]

In opposition to Columbus and Champlain, botanist, writer, and traveler William Bartram did not view the colonial landscape with an exploitative, ambitious eye. Rather, he used it to fulfill his spiritual needs. Using the wilderness as a symbol of purity and goodness, Bartram journeyed extensively through the southern colonies in the years immediately preceding the American Revolution, vividly and poetically detailing his findings in a travel log. The publication of his romanticized accounts of the colonial wilderness influenced many European thinkers and writers with its positive representations of the landscape and its promise of renewal and freshness. Bartram depicts himself as feeling com-

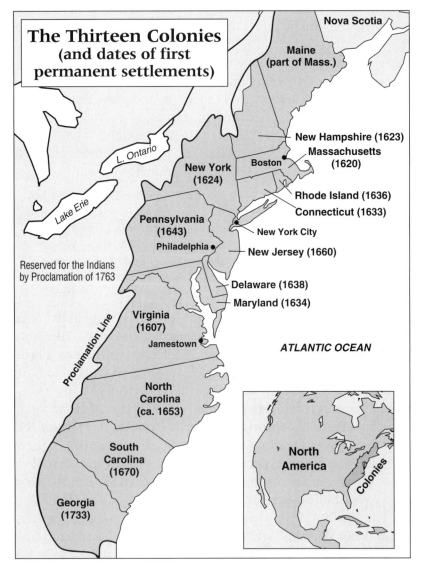

The Thirteen Colonies (and dates of first permanent settlements)

- Nova Scotia
- Maine (part of Mass.)
- New Hampshire (1623)
- Massachusetts (1620)
- Boston
- New York (1624)
- L. Ontario
- Lake Erie
- Rhode Island (1636)
- Connecticut (1633)
- Pennsylvania (1643)
- New York City
- Philadelphia
- New Jersey (1660)
- Reserved for the Indians by Proclamation of 1763
- Delaware (1638)
- Maryland (1634)
- Proclamation Line
- Virginia (1607)
- Jamestown
- ATLANTIC OCEAN
- North Carolina (ca. 1653)
- South Carolina (1670)
- North America
- Colonies
- Georgia (1733)

fortable with the solitude and vastness of the landscape, often setting "off alone and run[ning] all risks."[5] Author and critic Edward Abbey observes that "Bartram portrays a native scene where (almost) every prospect pleases and (only) European man is vile. . . . For Bartram, these were Elysian fields."[6] And reflecting one common European interpretation of the wilderness, Bartram ascribes the condition of the sublime (the belief that through experience/contemplation of a natural scene, the self and spirit can be elevated) to the American landscape:

> I approached a charming vale, amidst sublimely high forests, awful shades! Darkness gathers around; far distant thunder rolls over the trembling hills: the black clouds with august majesty and power, move slowly forwards, shading regions of towering hills, and threatening all destruction of thunderstorm: all around is now still as death, not a whisper is heard, but a total inactivity and silence seem to pervade the earth.[7]

Here, Bartram's experience with an imposing, dangerous, and beautiful act of nature removes him from the earthly realm and places him in a position from which he can gain spiritual knowledge about himself and the world that surrounds him. Descriptions like these, and the possibility for personal growth that they offer, are part of what captivated European colonists and motivated them to seek out the offerings of the New World.

The writings of Christopher Columbus, Samuel de Champlain, and William Bartram reflect many of the romantic views of the colonial landscape held by the European imagination. These writings and ideals encouraged the settlement and development of the New World, with readers embracing the dreams of personal fame and fortune, the unending natural beauty and resources, and the purity that the wilderness lands symbolized. Their travel logs testify to the characteristic American spirit of exploration and individuality and provide testaments to the dreams and imaginations that informed the development of the American colonies.

Notes

1. Christopher Columbus, *Digest of Columbus' Log-Book on His First Voyage*, in *Constructing Nature: Readings from the American Experience*, eds. Richard Jenseth and Edward E. Lotto. Upper Saddle River, NJ: Prentice-Hall, 1996, p. 9.

2. Quoted in Columbus, *Digest of Columbus' Log-Book on His First Voyage*, p. 9.

3. Samuel de Champlain, *The Voyages of Samuel de Champlain, 1604–1618*, in *The Harper American Literature*, vol. 2, ed. Donald McQuade. New York: Harper, 1994, p. 94.

4. Wallace Stegner, "The Twilight of Self-Reliance: Frontier Values and Contemporary America," in *Rereading America: Cultural Contexts for Critical Thinking and Writing*, 5th ed., Gary Colombo. Boston: Bedford, 2001, p. 701.

5. William Bartram, *The Travels of William Bartram*, in *Constructing Nature: Readings from the American Experience*, eds. Richard Jenseth and Edward E. Lotto. Upper Saddle River, NJ: Prentice-Hall, 1996, p. 52.

6. Edward Abbey, *Appalachian Wilderness*. New York: Arrowood, 1988, pp. 54, 59.

7. Quoted in Bartram, *The Travels of William Bartram*, p. 58.

Different Cultures, Different Values

CHAPTER 1

Chapter Preface

Several distinct cultures and peoples arrived in the American colonies from across the Atlantic Ocean. Often displacing the native Indian cultures that already existed on the continent, European settlements burgeoned beginning in the second half of the seventeenth century. The different groups of colonists established communities in the New World for different reasons, and their ways of life, influenced by their old traditions and the climate in their regions, differed drastically.

The Puritans, the first colonists to arrive in the Americas in 1621, fled religious persecution in Europe and established settlements along the rocky northern coast of New England. Tempered by rocky soil, desperately bleak winters, and poor agricultural conditions, the Puritans relied heavily on industry and subsistence-level farming for their livelihoods. Fueled by a strong sense of Christian piety, Puritan New Englanders sought to live highly moralistic and industrious lives in the service of God. To modern sensibilities, their religious beliefs appear oppressive and overly strict. Yet though they knew hardship and toil and found themselves in the middle of a dangerous wilderness, their religious faith kept them motivated.

The Dutch largely founded and populated the middle colonies of Pennsylvania, New York, and New Jersey. Unlike New England, the middle colonies were created primarily for monetary reasons. The communities were strategically placed in areas, such as Manhattan Island, that had fewer hardships than did their neighbors to the north. Originally drawn by the financial rewards of the fur and timber trade, the middle colonies nonetheless became an asylum for religious dissidents in Europe. The Quakers, led by William Penn, were welcomed neither in England nor in New England because of their differing religious convictions. Yet they went on to form their own prosperous and cosmopolitan culture, with the city of Philadelphia being the central symbol of their endeavors.

The first settlements in the South, beginning with the Jamestown colony of Virginia, like those in New England, were crude and endured innumerable difficulties during the first seasons. However, the lifestyles of the European settlers developed well, thanks in part to the character of the region. The southern colonies, blessed with a temperate climate and fertile soil, prospered economically. They capitalized on the overseas demand for cotton and tobacco and set up enormous plantations to grow these staple crops. Slaves taken from Africa performed much of the work on southern plantations. Their cultural heritage was forever changed and disrupted by the slave trade, illustrating a darker side to colonial history and southern culture.

Although the lifestyles and cultures in these distinct areas had their limitations and benefits, they reflected the individuality, conviction, diversity, and determined attitude that continue to define American life in contemporary times. As these settlements suggest, since colonial times the Americas have been envisioned as places of religious, political, and financial freedom unavailable in Europe.

Life in the Colonial Countryside

St. John de Crèvecoeur

St. John de Crèvecoeur traveled throughout the American colonies as a surveyor and trader in the eighteenth century, eventually purchasing a farm in New York State in 1769. His love for the American land and spirit is evident in his writings celebrating the Americas and comparing and contrasting them to the European soil and people. In the following selection, composed in the form of a letter, the author writes to those Europeans curious about the colonies and interested in moving to, investing in, or visiting the new lands. Crèvecoeur discusses the hardships and joys inherent to rural life in the colonies, making distinctions between the climates and character of the different colonial regions.

I am perfectly sensible of the superiority of your agriculture. England surpasses all the world for the perfection of mechanism and the peculiar excellence with which all its tools and implements are finished. We are but children and they [the English] our parents. The immense difference, therefore, ought not to make us blush. We have the same blood in our veins. In time we shall arrive likewise at perfection. All the praises we at present deserve ought to be bestowed on that strength, fortitude, and perseverance which have been requisite to clear so many fields, to drain so many swamps. Great parts of the colony of Massachusetts and Connecticut have cost more in clearing than the land was worth. The native industry of the English is nowhere more manifest than in the settlement and cultivation of those two provinces. They had every species of difficulty to struggle with: climate, stubbornness of soil, amazing trees, stones, etc. And yet now some parts of these countries, I am informed, are not inferior to the best cultivated spots in Europe, considering the short space of time in which these great works have been accomplished.

St. John de Crèvecoeur, *Sketches of Eighteenth Century America*. New Haven, CT: Yale University Press, 1925.

However inferior in all these rural respects we are to England, yet you seem to confess with pleasure the surprise you felt in travelling from New Hampshire to this place. Everywhere you saw good houses, well-fenced fields, ample barns, large orchards. Everywhere you saw the people busy either at home or on their farms. Everywhere they seemed contented and happy. You no sooner quitted the sight of an orchard, but another presented itself to your view. Everywhere tolerable roads, pretty towns, good bridges forced you to ask yourself: When is it that these people have had time and abilities to perform so many labours? Everywhere you inform me that you met with the most cordial hospitality. Tell me in what part of Europe you could have travelled three hundred and sixty miles for four dollars? I feel proud and happy that the various accounts I gave you of this part of America did not fall short of what you have experienced. The people of New England had been represented to you in a strange light, yet I know no province which is so justly entitled to the respect of the world on many accounts. They are the true and unmixed descendants of Englishmen, and surely there is no country in America where an Englishman ought to travel with more pleasure. Here he may find the names of almost all the towns in his country and those of many families with which he is acquainted.

Some people without knowing why look with disdain on their democratic government. They do not consider that this was the very rule which prevailed in England when they left it, and that nothing more than the blessings it confers could possibly have animated these people and urged them on to undertake such labours. Slaves may cultivate the smooth and fertile plains of the South. It is the hands of freemen only that could till this asperous soil. Had they laboured under an oppressive form of government, it is very probable that Massachusetts and Connecticut would have been possessed yet by the Pequots, the Narragansetts, and the Wampanoags, the ancient lords of these rough countries. There is not a province in the whole continent which does not exhibit to the contemplative traveller something highly praiseworthy and highly deserving the attention of a stranger. Everywhere you find the strongest marks of industry, of activity, and of prosperous boldness. When an Englishman arrives here he should quit his insular prejudices. He should procure a small book wherein he should carefully set down the date of every establishment, and thus furnished, he might travel with more satisfaction to himself and do more justice to the inhabitants. This is the rule I always observe. For instance, who can visit some of the modern settlements in the New Hampshire grants without amazement and surprise? I know many townships that are but twelve years old which contain inhabitants worth two thousand pounds, all acquired by their labours and good contrivance in that short space of time. The English farmer, when he purchases his farm, finds it already cleared, already fenced, already ditched. His ploughs are excellent; his horses good; his servants humble and subordinate. No wonder indeed that he can perform all the operations with so much neatness and accuracy! . . .

Treatment of Servants and Field Hands

As to labour and labourers,—what difference! When we hire any of these people we rather pray and entreat them. You must give them what they ask: three shillings per day in common wages and five or six shillings in harvest. They must be at your table and feed, as you saw it at my house, on the best you have. I have often seen Irishmen just landed, inconceivably hard to please and as greedy as wolves. These are a few of the many reasons why we can't bring anything to perfection. The few negroes we have are at best but our friends and companions. Their original cost is very high. Their clothing and their victuals amount to a great sum besides the risk of losing them. Our mechanics and tradesmen are very dear and sometimes great bunglers. Our winters are so severe and so long that we are obliged to consume during that season a great part of what we earn in the summer. This is, sir, but a feeble sketch of that great picture I might draw of the amazing inconveniences to which the locality of our situation exposes us.

Last year Mr. ———, the first man in our country, our first judge and assemblyman, received in harvest a large company from the town of ———. He immediately ordered two tables in two different rooms, for he always eats with his work-people. The reapers, perceiving the new distinction which he was going to establish, quitted him after having made very severe reflections, and it was not without great difficulties that he was enabled to finish his harvest with his own people. What would one of your country squires say to this? Whether this gentleman was entitled to the appellation or not, I cannot tell, but sure I am that he possesses fifteen hundred acres of excellent land and [belongs to] one of the most respectable families we have. We should be too happy were it otherwise. And indeed the present constitution of things: our government, modes of religion, our manners, the scarcity of people, the ease with which they may live and have lands of their own,—all these reasons must necessarily tend to subject us to these inconveniences. Better put up with them than with high taxes, encroachment of lords, free passage of hounds and huntsmen, tithes, etc.

Farm Life in the Colonies

Farming in the northern provinces is, therefore, not so advantageous as a European might at first imagine. These are fit only for people who are capable of working; the southern ones for those who have capital and can purchase negroes. I could mention to you a thousand other details, but they would be useless and perhaps tiresome. The proper distinction of ranks in England procures to the rich servants who know their places; to the farmers workmen who are afraid of losing their bread. Very different is our lot. A particular friend of mine who possesses a large farm and mows every year about one hundred and twenty acres of meadow, and keeps one hundred head of horned cattle, sheep, and horses in proportion, came the other day to dine with me. "How happily, how peaceably you live here," he said. "Your farm is not so large as mine and yet brings you all you want. You have time to rest and to think. For my part, I am weary. I must be in the fields with the hired men; nothing is done except I am there. I must not find fault with them or else they will quit me and give me a bad name. I am but the first slave on my farm." Nor is his case uncommon; it is that of every person who tills the earth upon a large scale. This gentleman's farm in Europe would constitute him an opulent man without giving himself any trouble besides a general oversight of the whole. . . .

I hope that in your travels through Virginia you'll find some planter who will inform you of every detail relating to their mode of planting. You'll then possess the two extremes and be better able to judge in what part it will be best for your friends to come and settle. Here we enjoy a happy poverty and a strong health. There riches are attainable, but the necessary intemperance of the climate leads to many diseases which northern farmers are strangers to. The good is always mixed with the evil. The matter is how to choose the least. Were I to begin the world again, I would go and pitch my tent either in a severe climate where the frost is never interrupted by pernicious thaws, or else at the foot of the Alleghenies where they almost enjoy a perpetual summer. Either of these extremes would suit me better than the climate of these middle colonies. Give me either a Canadian or a Mohawk winter, or else none at all.

Threats and Inconveniences to the Agricultural Community

Nor have I related you the tenth part of the inconveniences to which we are subject. Our country teems with more destructive insects and animals than Europe. 'Tis difficult for us to guard against them all. What man sows must be done here as well as everywhere else at the sweat of his brows, and here he has many more enemies to defend himself from than you have in Europe. The great woods with which our country is replenished affords them a shelter from which we cannot drive them. Such is the nature of man's labours and that of the grain he lives on that he is obliged to declare war against every ancient inhabitant of this country. Strange state of things! First by trials, by fraud, by a thousand artifices he drives away the ancient inhabitants. Then he is obliged to hunt the bear, the wolf, and the fox. The bear loves his apples, often climbs into our trees, and by his weight tears their limbs. The wolves, finding the deer becoming scarce, have learned how to feed on our sheep. The fox, for want of pheasants and partridges, lives on our poultry; the squirrels on our corn. The crows and the blackbirds know how to eradicate it out of the ground, even when it is four inches high. Caterpillars, an awful progeny, sometimes spontaneously arise in some countries and travel in quest of their particular food. Some attack the black oak, on the leaves of which they feed and entirely destroy them. Others attack our grass, eat every leaf, and leave nothing but the bare stalk. Others again spring up from the ground in imitation of the locust and enter into the heart of our corn, blasting the hopes of the farmer. Others climb into our apple trees and, if not prevented, eat all their leaves and buds and blossoms and render a flourishing orchard a sad picture of ruin, sterility, and desolation. At other times innumerable swarms of grasshoppers arise and indiscriminately feed on all they find; grain, grass, turnips, etc. I had once a field of four acres of hemp seven feet high, which they entirely stripped of all the leaves and rendered useless, whereby I lost at least a ton of that commodity.

Man sows and tills, and Nature from her great lap of fecundity often produces those swarms of beings, those great exuberances of life, which seem to threaten us with destruction. If these were general and not transitory, man would soon fall a victim to their devouring jaws, and, small as they are, they become by their numbers powerful agents of desolation. I have heard many people call them the avengers of the Almighty, created to punish men for their iniquities. This cannot be, for they eat the substance of the good and the wicked indiscriminately. They appear in certain districts or follow certain courses which they invariably pursue. What greater crimes do we commit than the Europeans? It is a local evil, and this evil is nothing among us to what you'll observe in the southern provinces. The heat and the moisture of their climates spread everywhere a disposition in matter to form itself into organized bodies. There their fields teem with ten thousand different species with which I am not acquainted. Strange that you should have in England so many learned and wise men, and that none should ever have come over here to describe some part of this great field which nature presents. I have heard several Virginians say that when their wheat is ripe a peculiar sort of winged weevil attacks it in the fields. The heads of this grain seem all alive, and it is with the utmost difficulty that they can save it. When in the barn, it becomes subject to the depredations of another sort [of insect] which, though deprived of wings, is equally terrible in the mischief it causes. Our very peas are subject to the attack of a fly which deposits an egg, imperceptible in the middle of its blossoms. This egg grows with the peas, which serve him as a cradle, but he does not touch them until towards the spring. Then he has acquired a degree of strength sufficient to eat the meat of the two lobes. The fly then bores a hole through which it quits its ancient habitation. The peas, reduced to this hollow state, will grow again, but are unfit for any culinary uses. There is no other remedy but to place them as soon as threshed in an oven half heated. The heat will parch and kill the worms.

Now if you unite the damages which we yearly suffer from all these enemies, to the badness of our fences, to the want of subordinate workmen, to the high price of our labour, to the ignorance of our tradesmen, to the severities of our winters, to the great labours we must undergo, to the celerity with which the rapid seasons hurry all our rural operations, you'll have a more complete idea of our situation as farmers than you had before. Some part of the rich landscape will gradually fail, and you'll soon perceive that the lot of the American farmer is very often unjustly envied by many Europeans who wish to see us taxed, and think that we live too well. It is true that no people feed on better pork and bread, but these are in general dearly earned.

He that is just arrived and sees a fine, smooth plantation with a good house or a flourishing orchard, and hears that the proprietor pays but a small tax, immediately thinks: this man is too happy. His imagination presents him with such images and ideas as are suggested to him by what he has seen in Europe. He sees not that sea of trouble, of labour, and expense which have been lavished on this farm. He forgets the fortitude, and the regrets with which the first emigrant left his friends, his relations, and his native land. He is unacquainted with the immense difficulties of first settlement, with the sums borrowed, with the many years of interest paid, with the various shifts these first people have been obliged to make use of. The original log-house, the cradle of the American, is now gone, and has made room for the more elegant framed one. Is there no credit to be given to these first cultivators who by their sweat, their toil, and their perseverance have come over a sea of three thousand miles to till a new soil? Thereby they have enlarged the trade, the power, the riches of the mother country. . . .

A Vision of American Self-Sufficiency

[The American farmers'] cheerful glass, the warmth of their country politics, the ruddy faces of their daughters, the goodness of their horses would give you a more lively idea of their happiness as men, of their native pride as free-holders than anything I could tell you. At these assemblies they forget all their cares, all their labours. They bring their governors and assemblymen to a severe account; they boldly blame them or censure them for such measures as they dislike. Here you might see the American freeman in all the latitude of his political felicity, a felicity—alas!— of which they are not so sensible as they ought to be. Your picture of the poor Germans and Russians makes me shudder. It is, then, to England we owe this elevated rank we possess, these noble appellations of freemen, freeholders, citizens; yes, it is to that wise people we owe our freedom. Had we been planted by some great monarchy, we should have been but the mean slaves of some distant monarch. Our great distance from him would have constituted the only happiness we should enjoy.

The small present of maple sugar which my wife sends you by this opportunity obliges me to [describe] to you another pleasurable scene in which I always spend a week or ten days every spring. In clearing his farm my father very prudently saved all the maple trees he found, which fortunately are all placed together in the middle of our woodland; and by his particular caution in bleeding them, they yield sap as plentifully as ever. The common method is to notch them with an axe. This operation, after a few years, destroys the tree entirely. That which my father followed is much easier, and gives these trees wounds which are almost imperceptible. The best time to make this sugar is between the months of March and April, according to the season. There must be snow on the ground, and it must freeze at night and thaw in the day. These three circumstances are absolutely requisite to make the sap run in abundance. But as my trees are but a little way from my house, I now and then go to try them, and, as soon as the time is come, then I bring all my hands, and we go to work. Nothing can be simpler than this operation. I previously provide myself with as many trays as I have trees. These I bore with a large gimlet. I then fix a spile made of elder through which the sap runs into the trays. From them it is carried into the boiler which is already fixed on the fire. If the evaporation is slow, we are provided with barrels to receive it. In a little time it becomes of the consistency of syrup. Then it is put into another vessel and made to granulate. When in that state we cast it into little moulds made according to the fancy of the farmer. Some persons know how to purify it, and I am told that there are people at Montreal who excel in this branch. For my part, I am perfectly well satisfied with the colour and taste which Nature has given it. When the trees have ceased to run we stop the holes with pegs made of the same wood. We cut them close to the bark, and in a little time the cicatrice becomes imperceptible. By these simple means our trees will afford sugar for a long time, nor have I ever observed that it impaired their growth in the least degree. They will run every year, according to the seasons, from six to fifteen days until their buds fill. They do not yield every year the same quantity, but as I regularly bleed two hundred trees, which are all I have, I have commonly received six barrels of sap in twenty-four hours which have yielded me from twelve to eighteen [pounds of sugar].

Thus without the assistance of the West Indies, by the help of my trees and of my bees, we yearly procure the sweetening we want; and it is not a small quantity, you know, that satisfies the wants of a tolerable American family. I have several times made sugar with the sap of the birch; though it seldom runs in any quantity, it is sweeter, richer, and makes stronger sugar. These trees, however, are so rare among us that they are never made use of for that purpose. By way of imitating in some respects my provident father, who so religiously saved this small sugar plan-tation, I have cleared about a half acre of land adjoining it, on which I have planted above seventy young maples, which I have raised in a nursery. As that part of my woods is extremely moist, I propose to enlarge this useful plantation as fast as I can raise trees big enough for transplantation.

Life Among the Native Americans

James Seaver

In the following selection, writer James Seaver relates a story dictated to him by Mary Jemison, a white woman who was captured by Native Americans as a girl in Philadelphia in 1758. Despite her initial terror at her capture and the murder of her parents, Jemison explains that she grew to enjoy her life among the Indians, where she married and had a child. She describes the Indian way of life as peaceful and simple, consisting of cultivating corn in the summers and hunting in the winters. She also insists that the cruelties inflicted by Indians are aimed only at their enemies and are based on their conception of justice.

I got home with the horse very early in the morning, where I found a man that lived in our neighborhood, and his sister-in-law who had three children, one son and two daughters. . . .

Immediately after I got home, the man took the horse to go to his house after a bag of grain, and took his gun in his hand for the purpose of killing game, if he should chance to see any.—Our family, as usual, was busily employed about their common business. Father was shaving an axe-helve at the side of the house; mother was making preparations for breakfast;—my two oldest brothers were at work near the barn; and the little ones, with myself, and the woman and her three children, were in the house.

Breakfast was not yet ready, when we were alarmed by the discharge of a number of guns, that seemed to be near. Mother and the women before mentioned, almost fainted at the report, and every one trembled with fear. On opening the door, the man and horse lay dead near the house, having just been shot by the Indians.

I was afterwards informed, that the Indians discovered him at his own house with his gun, and pursued him to father's, where

James Seaver, *A Narrative of the Life of Mary Jemison*. New York: Miller, Orton, and Mulligan, 1856.

they shot him as I have related. They first secured my father, and then rushed into the house, and without the least resistance made prisoners of my mother, Robert, Matthew, Betsey, the woman and her three children, and myself, and then commenced plundering.

My two brothers, Thomas and John, being at the barn, escaped and went to Virginia, where my grandfather Erwin then lived, as I was informed by a Mr. Fields, who was at my house about the close of the revolutionary war.

The party that took us consisted of six Indians and four Frenchmen, who immediately commenced plundering, as I just observed, and took what they considered most valuable; consisting principally of bread, meal and meat. Having taken as much provision as they could carry, they set out with their prisoners in great haste, for fear of detection, and soon entered the woods. . . .

Towards evening we arrived at the border of a dark and dismal swamp, which was covered with small hemlocks, or some other evergreen, and other bushes, into which we were conducted; and having gone a short distance we stopped to encamp for the night.

Here we had some bread and meat for supper: but the dreariness of our situation; together with the uncertainty under which we all labored, as to our future destiny, almost deprived us of the sense of hunger, and destroyed our relish for food. . . .

Parting Words

As soon as I had finished my supper, an Indian took off my shoes and stockings and put a pair of moccasins on my feet, which my mother observed; and believing that they would spare my life, even if they should destroy the other captives, addressed me as near as I can remember in the following words:—

"My dear little Mary, I fear that the time has arrived when we must be parted forever. Your life, my child, I think will be spared; but we shall probably be tomahawked here in this lonesome place by the Indians. O! how can I part with you my darling? What will become of my sweet little Mary? Oh! how can I think of your being continued in captivity without a hope of your being rescued? O that death had snatched you from my embraces in your infancy; the pain of parting then would have been pleasing to what it now is; and I should have seen the end of your troubles!—Alas, my dear! my heart bleeds at the thoughts of what awaits you; but, if you leave us, remember my child your own name, and the name of your father and mother. Be careful and not forget your English tongue. If you shall have an opportunity to get away from the Indians, don't try to escape; for if you do they will find and destroy you. Don't forget, my little daughter, the prayers that I have learned you—say them often; be a good child, and God will bless you. May God bless you my child, and make you comfortable and happy."

During this time, the Indians stripped the shoes and stockings from the little boy that belonged to the woman who was taken with us, and put moccasins on his feet, as they had done before on mine. I was crying. An Indian took the little boy and myself by the hand, to lead us off from the company, when my mother exclaimed, "Don't cry Mary—don't cry my child. God will bless you! Farewell—farewell!"

The Indian led us some distance into the bushes, or woods, and there lay down with us to spend the night. The recollection of parting with my tender mother kept me awake, while the tears constantly flowed from my eyes. A number of times in the night the little boy begged of me earnestly to run away with him and get clear of the Indians; but remembering the advice I had so lately received, and knowing the dangers to which we should be exposed, in travelling without a path and without a guide, through a wilderness unknown to us, I told him that I would not go, and persuaded him to lie still till morning.

Early the next morning the Indians and Frenchmen that we had left the night before, came to us; but our friends were left behind. It is impossible for any one to form a correct idea of what my feelings were at the sight of those savages, whom I supposed had murdered my parents and brothers, sister, and friends, and left them in the swamp to be devoured by wild beasts! But what could I do? A poor little defenceless girl; without the power or means of escaping; without a home to go to, even if I could be liberated; without a knowledge of the direction or distance to my former place of residence; and without a living friend to whom to fly for protection, I felt a kind of horror, anxiety, and dread, that, to me, seemed insupportable. I durst not cry—I durst not complain; and to inquire of them the fate of my friends (even if I could have mustered resolution) was beyond my ability, as I could not speak their language, nor they understand mine. My only relief was in silent stifled sobs.

Days of Marching

My suspicions as to the fate of my parents proved too true; for soon after I left them they were killed and scalped, together with Robert, Matthew, Betsey, and the woman and her two children, and mangled in the most shocking manner.

Having given the little boy and myself some bread and meat for breakfast, they led us on as fast as we could travel, and one of them went behind and with a long staff, picked up all the grass and weeds that we trailed down by going over them. By taking that precaution they avoided detection; for each weed was so nicely placed in its natural position that no one would have suspected that we had passed that way. . . .

They made me to understand that they should not have killed the family if the whites had not pursued them.

Mr. Fields, whom I have before mentioned, informed me that at the time we were taken, he lived in the vicinity of my father; and that on hearing of our captivity, the whole neighborhood turned out in pursuit of the enemy, and to deliver us if possible: but that their efforts were unavailing. They however pursued us to the dark swamp, where they found my father, his family and companions, stripped and mangled in the most inhuman manner: That from thence the march of the cruel monsters could not be traced in any direction; and that they returned to their homes with the melancholy tidings of our misfortunes, supposing that we had all shared in the massacre.

The next morning we went on; the Indian going behind us and setting up the weeds as on the day before. At night we encamped on the ground in the open air, without a shelter or fire.

In the morning we again set out early, and travelled as on the two former days, though the weather was extremely uncomfortable, from the continual falling of rain and snow.

At night the snow fell fast, and the Indians built a shelter of boughs, and a fire, where we rested tolerably dry through that and the two succeeding nights. . . .

On account of the storm, we were two days at that place. On one of those days, a party consisting of six Indians who had been to the frontier settlements, came to where we were, and brought with them one prisoner, a young white man who was very tired and dejected. His name I have forgotten.

Misery certainly loves company. I was extremely glad to see him, though I knew from his appearance, that his situation was as deplorable as mine, and that he could afford me no kind of assistance. In the afternoon the Indians killed a deer, which they dressed, and then roasted it whole; which made them a full meal. We were each allowed a share of their venison, and some bread, so that we made a good meal also.

Having spent three nights and two days at that place, and the storm having ceased, early in the morning the whole company, consisting of twelve Indians, four Frenchmen, the young man, the little boy and myself, moved on at a moderate pace without an Indian behind us to deceive our pursuers.

In the afternoon we came in sight of Fort Pitt (as it is now called), where we were halted while the Indians performed some customs upon their prisoners which they deemed necessary. That fort was then occupied by the French and Indians, and was called Fort Du Quesne. . . .

A Gloomy Night

At the place where we halted, the Indians combed the hair of the young man, the boy and myself, and then painted our faces and hair red, in the finest Indian style. We were then conducted into the fort, where we received a little bread, and were then shut up and left to tarry alone through the night. . . .

The night was spent in gloomy forebodings. What the result of our captivity would be, it was out of our power to determine or even imagine.—At times we could almost realize the approach of our masters to butcher and scalp us;—again we could nearly see the pile of wood kindled on which we were to be roasted; and then we would imagine ourselves at liberty; alone and defenceless in the forest, surrounded by wild beasts that were ready to devour us. The anxiety of our minds drove sleep from our eyelids; and it was with a dreadful hope and painful impatience that we waited for the morning to determine our fate.

The morning at length arrived, and our masters came early and let us out of the house, and gave the young man and boy to the French, who immediately took them away. Their fate I never learned; as I have not seen nor heard of them since.

I was now left alone in the fort, deprived of my former companions, and of everything that was near or dear to me but life. But it was not long before I was in some measure relieved by the appearance of two pleasant looking squaws of the Seneca tribe, who came and examined me attentively for a short time, and then went out. After a few minutes absence they returned with my former masters, who gave me to them to dispose of as they pleased.

The Indians by whom I was taken were a party of Shawanees, if I remember right, that lived, when at home, a long distance down the Ohio.

Adoption

My former Indian masters, and the two squaws, were soon ready to leave the fort, and accordingly embarked; the Indians in a large canoe, and the two squaws and myself in a small one, and went down the Ohio. . . .

At night we arrived at a small Seneca Indian town, at the mouth of a small river, that was called by the Indians, in the Seneca language, She-nan-jee, where the two Squaws to whom I belonged resided. There we landed, and the Indians went on; which was the last I ever saw of them.

Having made fast to the shore, the Squaws left me in the canoe while they went to their wigwam or house in the town, and returned with a suit of Indian clothing, all new, and very clean and nice. My clothes, though whole and good when I was taken, were now torn in pieces, so that I was almost naked. They first undressed me and threw my rags into the river; then washed me clean and dressed me in the new suit they had just brought, in complete Indian style; and then led me home and seated me in the center of their wigwam.

I had been in that situation but a few minutes, before all the Squaws in the town came in to see me. I was soon surrounded by them, and they immediately set up a most dismal howling, crying bitterly, and wringing their hands in all the agonies of grief for a deceased relative.

Their tears flowed freely, and they exhibited all the signs of real mourning. At the commencement of this scene, one of their number began, in a voice somewhat between speaking and singing, to recite some words to the following purport, and continued the recitation till the ceremony was ended; the company at the same time varying the appearance of their countenances, gestures and tone of voice, so as to correspond with the sentiments expressed by their leader:

"Oh our brother! Alas! He is dead—he has gone; he will never return! Friendless he died on the field of the slain, where his bones are yet lying unburied! Oh, who will not mourn his sad fate? No tears dropped around him; oh, no! No tears of his sisters were there! He fell in his prime, when his arm was most needed to keep us from danger! Alas! he has gone! and left us in sorrow, his loss to bewail: Oh where is his spirit? His spirit went naked, and hungry it wanders, and thirsty and wounded it groans to return! Oh helpless and wretched, our brother has gone! No blanket nor food to nourish and warm him; nor candles to light him, nor weapons of war;—Oh, none of those comforts had he! But well we remember his deeds!—The deer he could take on the chase! The panther shrunk back at the sight of his strength! His enemies fell at his feet! He was brave and courageous in war! As the fawn he was harmless: his friendship was ardent: his temper was gentle: his pity was great! Oh! our friend, our companion is dead! Our brother, our brother, alas! he is gone! But why do we grieve for his loss? In the strength of a warrior, undaunted he left us, to fight by the side of the Chiefs! His war-whoop was shrill! His rifle well aimed laid his enemies low: his tomahawk drank of their blood: and his knife flayed their scalps while yet covered with gore! And why do we mourn? Though he fell on the field of the slain, with glory he fell, and his spirit went up to the land of his fathers in war! Then why do we mourn? With transports of joy they received him, and fed him, and clothed him, and welcomed him there! Oh friends, he is happy; then dry up your tears! His spirit has seen our distress, and sent us a helper whom with pleasure we greet. Dickewamis has come: then let us receive her with joy! She is handsome and pleasant! Oh! she is our sister, and gladly we welcome her here. In the place of our brother she stands in our tribe. With care we will guard her from trouble; and may she be happy till her spirit shall leave us."

In the course of that ceremony, from mourning they became serene—joy sparkled in their countenances, and they seemed to rejoice over me as over a long lost child. I was made welcome amongst them as a sister to the two Squaws before mentioned, and was called Dickewamis; which being interpreted, signifies a pretty girl, a handsome girl, or a pleasant, good thing. That is the name by which I have ever since been called by the Indians.

I afterwards learned that the ceremony I at that time passed through, was that of adoption. The two squaws had lost a brother in [George] Washington's war [the French and Indian War], sometime in the year before, and in consequence of his death went up to Fort Pitt, on the day on which I arrived there, in order to receive a prisoner or an enemy's scalp, to supply their loss.

It is a custom of the Indians, when one of their number is slain or taken prisoner in battle, to give to the nearest relative to the dead or absent, a prisoner, if they have chanced to take one, and if not, to give him the scalp of an enemy. On the return of the Indians from conquest, which is always announced by peculiar shoutings, demonstrations of joy, and the exhibition of some trophy of victory, the mourners come forward and make their claims. If they receive a prisoner, it is at their option either to satiate their vengeance by taking his life in the most cruel manner they can conceive of; or, to receive and adopt him into the family, in the place of him whom they have lost. All the prisoners that are taken in battle and carried to the encampment or town by the Indians, are given to the bereaved families, till their number is made good. And unless the mourners have but just received the news of their bereavement, and are under the operation of a paroxysm of grief, anger and revenge; or, unless the prisoner is very old, sickly, or homely, they generally save him, and treat him kindly. But if their mental wound is fresh, their loss so great that they deem it irreparable, or if their prisoner or prisoners do not meet their approbation, no torture, let it be ever so cruel, seems sufficient to make them satisfaction. It is family, and not national, sacrifices amongst the Indians, that has given them an indelible stamp as barbarians, and identified their character with the idea which is generally formed of unfeeling ferocity, and the most abandoned cruelty.

It was my happy lot to be accepted for adoption; and at the time of the ceremony I was received by the two squaws, to supply the place of their brother in the family; and I was ever considered and treated by them as a real sister, the same as though I had been born of their mother.

During my adoption, I sat motionless, nearly terrified to death at the appearance and actions of the company, expecting every moment to feel their vengeance, and suffer death on the spot. I was, however, happily disappointed, when at the close of the ceremony the company retired, and my sisters went about employing every means for my consolation and comfort.

An Easy Situation

Being now settled and provided with a home, I was employed in nursing the children, and doing light work about the house. Occasionally I was sent out with the Indian hunters, when they went but a short distance, to help them carry their game. My situation was easy; I had no particular hardships to endure. But still, the recollection of my parents, my brothers and sisters, my home, and my own captivity, destroyed my happiness, and made me constantly solitary, lonesome and gloomy.

My sisters would not allow me to speak English in their hearing; but remembering the charge that my dear mother gave me at the time I left her, whenever I chanced to be alone I made a business of repeating my prayer, catechism, or something I had learned in order that I might not forget my own language. By practicing in that way I retained it till I came to Genesee flats, where I soon became acquainted with English people with whom I have been almost daily in the habit of conversing.

My sisters were diligent in teaching me their language; and to their great satisfaction I soon learned so that I could understand it readily, and speak it fluently. I was very fortunate in falling into their hands; for they were kind good natured women; peaceable and mild in their dispositions; temperate and decent in their habits, and very tender and gentle towards me. I have great reason to respect them, though they have been dead a great number of years.

The town where they lived was pleasantly situated on the Ohio, at the mouth of the Shenanjee: the land produced good corn; the woods furnished a plenty of game, and the waters abounded with fish. Another river emptied itself into the Ohio, directly opposite the mouth of the Shenanjee. We spent the summer at that place, where we planted, hoed, and harvested a large crop of corn, of an excellent quality. . . .

The corn being harvested, the Indians took it on horses and in canoes, and proceeded down the Ohio, occasionally stopping to hunt a few days, till we arrived at the mouth of Sciota river; where they established their winter quarters, and continued hunting till the ensuing spring, in the adjacent wilderness. While at that place I went with the other children to assist the hunters to bring in their game. The forests on the Sciota were well stocked with elk, deer, and other large animals; and the marshes contained large numbers of beaver, muskrat, &c. which made excellent hunting for the Indians; who depended, for their meat, upon their success in taking elk and deer; and for ammunition and clothing, upon the beaver, muskrat, and other furs that they could take in addition to their peltry.

The season for hunting being passed, we all returned in the spring to the mouth of the river Shenanjee, to the houses and fields we had left in the fall before. There we again planted our corn, squashes, and beans, on the fields that we occupied the preceding summer. . . .

We tended our cornfields through the summer; and after we had harvested the crop, we again went down the river to the hunting ground on the Sciota, where we spent the winter, as we had done the winter before.

Early in the spring we sailed up the Ohio river, to a place that the Indians called Wiishto, where one river emptied into the Ohio on one side, and another on the other. At that place the Indians built a town, and we planted corn.

Family Life

We lived three summers at Wiishto, and spent each winter on the Sciota.

The first summer of our living at Wiishto, a party of Delaware Indians came up the river, took up their residence, and lived in common with us. . . .

Not long after the Delawares came to live with us, at Wiishto, my sisters told me that I must go and live with one of them, whose name was She-nin-jee. Not daring to cross them, or disobey their commands, with a great degree of reluctance I went; and Sheninjee and I were married according to Indian custom.

Sheninjee was a noble man; large in stature; elegant in his appearance; generous in his conduct; courageous in war; a friend to peace, and a great lover of justice. He supported a degree of dignity far above his rank, and merited and received the confidence and friendship of all the tribes with whom he was acquainted. Yet, Sheninjee was an Indian. The idea of spending my days with him, at first seemed perfectly irreconcilable to my feelings: but his good nature, generosity, tenderness, and friendship towards me, soon gained my affection; and, strange as it may seem, I loved him!—To me he was ever kind in sickness, and always treated me with gentleness; in fact, he was an agreeable husband, and a comfortable companion. . . .

In the second summer of my living at Wiishto, I had a child at the time that the kernels of corn first appeared on the cob. When I was taken sick, Sheninjee was absent, and I was sent to a small shed, on the bank of the river, which was made of boughs, where I was obliged to stay till my husband returned. My two sisters, who were my only companions, attended me, and on the second day of my confinement my child was born; but it lived only two days. It was a girl: and notwithstanding the shortness of the time that I possessed it, it was a great grief to me to lose it.

After the birth of my child, I was very sick, but was not allowed to go into the house for two weeks; when, to my great joy, Sheninjee returned, and I was taken in and as comfortably provided for as our situation would admit of. My disease continued to increase for a number of days; and I became so far reduced that my recovery was despaired of by my friends, and I concluded that my troubles would soon be finished. At length, however, my complaint took a favorable turn, and by the time that the corn was ripe I was able to get about. I continued to gain my health, and in the fall was able to go to our winter quarters, on the Sciota, with the Indians.

From that time, nothing remarkable occurred to me till the fourth winter of my captivity, when I had a son born, while I was at Sciota: I had a quick recovery, and my child was healthy. To commemorate the name of my much lamented father, I called my son Thomas Jemison. . . .

The Indian Mode of Living

I had then been with the Indians four summers and four winters, and had become so far accustomed to their mode of living, habits and dispositions, that my anxiety to get away, to be set at liberty, and leave them, had almost subsided. With them was my home; my family was there, and there I had many friends to whom I was warmly attached in consideration of the favors, affection and friendship with which they had uniformly treated me, from the time of my adoption. Our labor was not severe; and that of one year was exactly similar, in almost every respect, to that of the others, without that endless variety that is to be observed in the common labor of the white people. Notwithstanding the Indian women have all the fuel and bread to procure, and the cooking to perform, their task is probably not harder than that of white women, who have those articles provided for them; and their cares certainly are not half as numerous, nor as great. In the summer season, we planted, tended and harvested our corn, and generally had all our children with us; but had no master to oversee or drive us, so that we could work as leisurely as we pleased. We had no ploughs on the Ohio; but performed the whole process of planting and hoeing with a small tool that resembled, in some respects, a hoe with a very short handle.

Our cooking consisted in pounding our corn into samp or hommany, boiling the hommany, making now and then a cake and baking it in the ashes, and in boiling or roasting our venison. As our cooking and eating utensils consisted of a hommany block and pestle, a small kettle, a knife or two, and a few vessels of bark or wood, it required but little time to keep them in order for use.

Spinning, weaving, sewing, stocking and knitting, and the like, are arts which have never been practised in the Indian tribes generally. After the revolutionary war, I learned to sew, so that I could make my own clothing after a poor fashion; but the other domestic arts I have been wholly ignorant of the application of, since my captivity. In the season of hunting, it was our business, in addition to our cooking, to bring home the game that was taken by the Indians, dress it, and carefully preserve the eatable meat, and prepare or dress the skins. Our clothing was fastened together with strings of deer skin, and tied on with the same.

In that manner we lived, without any of those jealousies, quarrels, and revengeful battles between families and individuals, which have been common in the Indian tribes since the introduction of ardent spirits amongst them.

The use of ardent spirits amongst the Indians, and the attempts which have been made to civilize and christianize them by the white people, has constantly made them worse and worse; increased their vices, and robbed them of many of their virtues; and will ultimately produce their extermination. I have seen, in a number of instances, the effects of education upon some of our Indians, who were taken when young, from their families, and placed at school before they had had an opportunity to contract many Indian habits, and there kept till they arrived to manhood; but I have never seen one of those but what was an Indian in every respect after he returned. Indians must and will be Indians, in spite of all the means that can be used for their cultivation in the sciences and arts.

One thing only marred my happiness, while I lived with them on the Ohio; and that was the recollection that I had once had tender parents, and a home that I loved. Aside from that consideration, or, if I had been taken in infancy, I should have been contented in my situation. Notwithstanding all that has been said against the Indians, in consequence of their cruelties to their enemies—cruelties that I have witnessed, and had abundant proof of—it is a fact that they are naturally kind, tender and peaceable towards their friends, and strictly honest; and that those cruelties have been practised, only upon their enemies, according to their idea of justice.

The Slave's Life in Colonial America

Oscar Reiss

History scholar Oscar Reiss provides a succinct and straight-forward report on the day-to-day social activities of African American slaves throughout the American colonies. The author is an important academic voice in contemporary black studies whose work has been used in many college and high school classrooms. Reiss points out that slavery was practiced in all of the colonies and discusses the differing treatment of slaves from region to region. While Reiss focuses on everything from work habits to housing and nutrition, he constantly reminds the reader of the impact that forced enslavement had on black culture, pointing out the disruptions to family, community, and personal well-being that the slave system promoted.

L ike everything else in the slave's life, his living quarters were often described with a subjective rather than an objective view. One archaeological study provided a straightforward description of his "home." It was a one-room frame dwelling with a dirt floor which measured 17 by 20 feet. The cabin had at least one glazed and shuttered window. There was one door with a plate stock lock and a brick chimney with a dirt-floored brick hearth. This provided accommodations for seven or eight adults, with per-haps a sleeping loft for children. Digging in the earth floor brought up lead shot, gun flints, and percussion caps, which suggested that these inhabitants had access to firearms, legally or illegally. The cabin was built of logs without windows or floors. Crevices be-tween the logs allowed in light, cold, and rain. There was a door on wooden hinges. The cabin also had a fireplace for cooking and heating. According to Philip Foner, crevices between the logs were daubed with mud, and light and ventilation were provided by holes in the walls covered by wooden shutters. The chimney was built of mud and sticks, and caught fire frequently. Furniture was built or found by the cabin's inhabitants. Boxes were used for sitting or storage. Gourds, wooden buckets, and a wash barrel contained the water needed for cooking and washing. The occupants slept on planks with wooden pillows or on mattresses stuffed with corn husks. . . . On a very large plantation with many slaves, the slave quarters formed almost a small village. There were household cabins, workhouses, a children's house (nursery), a sick house and bachelor's quarters. The living accommodations of the "house slaves" were of better quality and close to the main house, so they could be available on short notice.

In the middle states and New England, where the farmer or wealthy urban dweller owned one or two humans, the slaves slept in the master's house, often in the loft with the master's children.

Clothing

Wearing apparel had to fit weather conditions. Johann Martin Bolzius, clergyman of the Salzburgers in Carolina and Georgia, described the slaves' clothing in a questionnaire sent to him from Germany. He claimed that blacks went naked in the summer, except that the men wore a cloth rag that hung down from a strap around the waist. Women had petticoats, but their upper bodies were bare. Children were totally naked. In the winter, they had shoes, and they wore a woolen blue or white camisole, cloth pants that reached to their shoes, a wool cap, but no shirt. Negroes who accompanied their master to town were dressed better, and skilled Negroes who lived in Charleston were well dressed. He believed it cost about 4 shillings to clothe a Negro each year. (The questionnaire was dated 1767.) In eighteenth-century South Carolina, slave clothing was stipulated by law, but this was not enforced. Fabric suitable for Negro clothing included Negro cloth duffels, osnaburgs (coarse linen of flax and tow), blue linen, check linen, coarse "garlix" [sic], coarse calicos, check cottons, and Scottish plaids. Favored male slaves were dressed in full livery and rode as attendants on painted coaches. (The specific types of cloth described in the law may have been a means of identifying runaway slaves.) As seen through the rose-colored glasses of [plantation slave owner] Schoolcraft, the clothing of

children and older Negroes was made by trained black seam-
stresses under the supervision of the mistress of the plantation.
The master bought planes, an all-wool cloth used by all the inhabitants of the plantation; this cost one dollar per yard. Slave
women wore a white shirt with a blue bodice; men wore white
pants and a blue coat. Women covered their heads with a red
kerchief or turban, while the men had red wool caps. According
to [scholars] Otto and Burns, summer wear was coarse cotton,
"jeans," and flannel. Slaves were given thread, needles, buttons,
scissors, and brass thimbles. Generally, clothing for men and boys
was the same as was the clothing for women and girls. They
wore coarse woolens in the winter and cotton in the summer.
They wore no underwear, and the men were not given shirts.
Strong shoes were supplied for winter wear.

In one case, the administrative council of a small community,
probably in Virginia, took up the problem of clothing a Negro
woman on October 19, 1692: "Whereas Mr. Ebenezer Taylor, late
schoolmaster. . . . It is thought reasonable that a negro woman
belonging to the sd. schoole should be clothed at the charges of
the Schoole master she being almost naked. It is therefore ordered that the sd Taylor provide . . . one new cotton waistcoat
and pettycoat, three yards of good new canvis for a shift, one
pare new shoon and stockins."

Food

The Puritan slaveholder in New England treated his Indian and
black bondsmen in the patriarchal manner described among the
Hebrews of the Old Testament. They were almost family members and ate at the common table. Similarly, the small farmer of
the middle colonies usually worked side by side with his slaves,
and their food intake was equal. The urban black was adequately
fed. He also had money that he earned and could buy any additional food and drink that he felt he needed. The plantation economy of the South was different. Often, as in the West Indies, land
was too valuable to grow foodstuffs, which had to be purchased.
If the slave depended on the master's largesse, he would develop
caloric and protein deficiencies. The basic food supplied to the
slave was Indian corn or yams. A working man or woman received a peck or two gallons of corn per week, distributed on Sun-

day. Working children received half this amount, and little children received about one quarter. In the Deep South, two pecks of unhusked rice was substituted for corn. Protein was supplied in the form of salt fish, salt beef, or salt bacon, approximately three and a half pounds per week. Each worker received a quart of salt each month. Occasionally, molasses was used to cut down the meat ration. According to the Reverend Bolzius, slaves were fed potatoes, unsold rice, Indian corn, and beans. Women and children received the same food in lesser amounts. An adult received 20 bushels of grain per year. Bolzius believed food cost per slave per year was 20 shillings. Schoolcraft, who saw the slave as a pet of his owner, said that every plantation had a butcher to kill animals: "When a great bullock is killed for negroes, they make 20 gallons of soup . . . and divide it." They received a food allowance weekly as "determined by law or experience." This included corn, rice, peas, sweet potatoes, molasses, fish, beef or bacon. All writers agreed that the slave had to return to his cabin after work, start a fire, grind his grain, and prepare his nightly meal. In addition, he prepared the food for two meals to be eaten the following day during 15-minute breaks from work. The cabin usually contained one cooking kettle, so everything was thrown in to create a stew; this was dished out into individual bowls. Occasionally, the master supplied his workers with ceramic dishes for their food. Grain was an important part of their diet. This was ground to produce a meal to which enough water was added to create a consistency that would support an upright spoon. A pat of this was positioned between oak leaves and placed in the ashes to produce "ash cake." When dropped on a hoe and baked, it was called "hoe-cake." Fortunately, the slave had the use of a piece of land to grow food to supplement his family's rations. He worked his land on Sundays and on holidays and after he had completed his assigned tasks for the plantation. On his plot, the bondsman grew cabbage, cauliflower, cowpeas (black-eyed peas), corn, turnip, and rutabagas. He also had chicken coops, rabbit hutches, and pigpens. The animals were fed from the slave's rations, and they were butchered for the slave's use, or they could be sold to merchants or to the slave's owner. According to Mrs. Schoolcraft, a plantation slave near the coast had a "canoe" made by hollowing out a log; at night, he could fish for prawn, crabs, clams, turtles, and fish. (That a plantation owner would allow a slave to have a boat is unlikely, particularly if the slaves knew about Spanish Florida to the south with its offer of liberty to escaped slaves.) . . .

The Slave System Disrupts Family Relationships

Slave marriages tended to be unstable and frequently were of short duration. As a group, the only slaveholders who took slaves' marriages seriously were the Puritans. Adultery was a serious sin and marriage a sanctified institution, even among bondsmen. A marriage ceremony was performed, and the participants were expected to stay together for life. If slaves were sold, the owner tried to sell them as a family unit. Among other groups, only a deeply religious master tried to promote morality and avoid licentiousness among his possessions. Under these conditions, slave unions could last a lifetime. The father then became an important part of the family, and he frequently worked nights and Sundays to provide his family with small "luxuries" like extra food and clothing. The children benefited by having a strong father figure in the cabin; however, this was an unusual situation. Statistically, 32.4 percent of 2,888 slave unions were dissolved by the master; the average marriage lasted about six years.

The typical slave marriage was not sanctified by a clergyman. In some cases, perhaps with a devoted house slave, a minister might be present, but he rarely performed the ceremony. The closest formality to marriage was "jumping the broom," with the promise that "you will cleave to him only, so long as God, in his Providence, shall continue his and your abode in such place (or places) as that you can come together." They were "married" until the master sold one partner away. In many states, the slave code prevented real marriage. A slave could not enter into a contract and marriage was a binding contract, so their marriage was called a contubernium, literally a sharing of the tent. The closest institution in society today would be that of the "significant other."

On large holdings, the master preferred that his slaves marry within the plantation. Marrying someone from another plantation meant that the "husband" would have to take time to walk over to see his wife. Also, the offspring of the union would belong to the wife's owner. Occasionally, to avoid lost time and progeny, a master would purchase his male's consort. The "husband" who visited his wife, usually for sexual gratification, was not considered a father figure by the offspring. The mother became the dominant figure in the slave family, and she provided for the children's needs. Very early in its life, the baby was turned over to its older siblings or to an "old woman" for care. The care of children by older siblings created an important bond—if the parents were sold away, the children could maintain a semblance of family. The damage produced by separating children from their mothers was recognized by state authorities. The Louisiana legislature, for example, prohibited separation of a mother from her child who was less than ten years. Like most humane legislation regarding slaves, unfortunately, this was not enforced.

Owners Encourage Problematic Behavior

Sexual promiscuity was encouraged by the owner. If a couple was not fertile, he separated them and gave each a new mate, because the purpose of "marriage" was the production of more slaves. A good "breeder" was a prized possession. If a slave union was broken by the sale of one spouse, the remaining individual was forced to take another sexual partner. Breeding was so important to the owner that he would push young girls of 13 into a relationship. In some areas, a woman with ten live children could receive her freedom; the children, however, would remain with her ex-master. The males' input into the breeding process was not overlooked. Strong, potent men were hired out as studs to other planters to produce a strong breed of children. In addition, the owner could take a comely slave at will, and the offspring of this "union" was added to his working population. In some situations, the white father accepted parental responsibility, and he educated and freed his child.

In the larger communities of the North, as well as on small farms, breeders were not prized. The problem was lack of space in the homes and inability to find a use for the children. Two classified advertisements in the *New York Mercury* bear this out: "June 3, 1765. To be sold a likely Negro wench, about 30 years old, with her two children, the elder a Girl between 3 and 4 years; the other a Boy about one year. She is a very good Conditioned Wench and can do all Manner of House Work: The only reason for selling her, is because she breeds; which her present Master and Mistress are adverse to; they being advanced in years." On December 12, 1765, this appeared: "A very likely Negro Wench, about 27 years old, with a Male child 5 months old: She is very handy, faithful and honest: sold for no fault but getting children."

The end product of the breeding process was the child, who belonged to the master. Generally, nursing was permitted for about three months. It was believed, as it is still in many quarters today, that nursing prevented pregnancy, and the master wanted his "machine" to reproduce as frequently as possible. However, removal of the child from his mother's breast exposed him to infantile diarrhea with its attendant mortality. If children survived the childhood illnesses and the diseases of poor nutrition and poorer hygiene, work was soon found for them. At five or six, they became messengers. They fanned the white family when they ate and acted as pages when the white family went out for a drive or visit. As the children aged, they were introduced to field work. They might start as water carriers to the adults working in the fields. They also attended the livestock, drove the wagons filled with produce out of the field, and kept crows out of the field by running, jumping, and screaming. . . .

Holidays and Celebrations: A Time for Community and Amusement

On Sunday the slave was relieved of his duty to his master. He could relax, go to church, or work on his own plot to earn extra money. In addition, there were two main periods of relaxation— summer lay-by and Christmas. The lay-by was at the end of the cultivation period when the bondsman's duties were decreased and he could work for himself. Christmas was a special holiday when the slave was free of all duty from three to six days. This period acted as a steam valve or cathartic to ease the tensions built up in a year of servitude. The owner encouraged license and unruliness with the hope that the slave population would then be more docile during the rest of the year. During the Christmas break, the slaves were occupied with the John Canoe (Jonkonnu) festivities. First recorded in America in 1774, this holiday came to the southern mainland from the Caribbean, and probably originally from the Guinea coast. The strongest male on the plantation dressed in bizarre clothes; wore ox horns on his head; covered his face with a mask; and placed boar tusks in his mouth. He danced around the festive site, followed by his retinue of "drunken women." The slaves frequently used the celebration for more serious activities. Under the cover of the festivities they stole to supplement their needs, made plans to run away and executed them, and prepared for insurrection. They also showed resentment of their servile state under the cover of comedy. The slave might use his "fancy" costume to mock the poor whites in the area. The activities were carried out by the field hands, because the house slaves abstained from the excitement—they saw themselves as a "higher class." The master seemed to enjoy the festivities, but he was fully aware of the undercurrents and tightened security on the plantation to avoid trouble.

During this period, individual planters provided feasts for their own slaves and those of neighboring plantations. The participants put on their best clothes and ate meats, vegetables, and other delicacies denied them during the rest of the year. Long tables were set in front of the main house; men sat on one side, women on the other. The meal was followed by dancing. Then the slaves visited the main house, where they received presents from the master. Mrs. Schoolcraft described the festivities: "The Negroes in the south are allowed three or four days every Christmas for a jubilee, and I so vividly remember the patriarchal benevolence, my father's countenance exhibited, when out of his abundant larder he contributed everything necessary to these jovial feastings among his slaves. Some of them spent the holy days in playing on the violins and other instruments, for their young friends to dance by; others went from place to place, to visit their neighbors, and others held prayer-meetings, where most of the night was spent in singing psalms in religious exhortations, and in prayer." In addition to Christmas, the slaves might be invited to partake in significant celebrations of the white family, such as birthdays or anniversaries.

The bottom line of the entire institution of slavery was profit derived from keeping humans at a subsistence level. In the eighteenth century, for the small farmer who could double his output with an additional pair of hands, or the small factory owner who owned or hired slaves at lower rates than white workers, a return on the investment was possible. In the cities, where slaves were used as cooks, butlers, and coachmen, the return was prestige rather than dollars. Slaveholding was important to the economic and social status of whites in the colonial period and remained a uniform measure of wealth during the Revolution because of the distortions produced by inflation. Wealth was measured in numbers of slaves rather than in money. For example the possession of 20 slaves in the pre-Revolutionary South made one a "man of means," a good-sized plantation had at least 70 slaves.

The plantation slave system gave the white owner freedom to gain additional schooling, to obtain military training, and to go into politics. This small elite group provided the leaders of the government in Southern states. As Mrs. Schoolcraft explained, "The exemption from manual labor supplied by slaves of South Carolina to the sons and daughters of Carolina forms one of the chief characteristics of southern life. It produces a class of elevation and refinement not achieved under any other system. This caused the filling of this colony with gentlemen of aristocratic taste and refinement." Their lifestyle resembled that of the nobility of Europe, and, like their European counterparts, they were in debt to the lower class merchants and traders. . . .

Among these "aristocrats" the highest individuals were the body servants. At the top of the pyramid was the "black mammy." She cared for the young white children, and was second in command to the mistress. A child raised by a mammy had the cachet of aristocracy. She was practically a part of the family, and her ideals were those of the whites. Unlike other slave women, she was considered self-respecting, independent, loyal, forward, gentle, "captious," affectionate, true, strong, just, warm-hearted, compassionate, and fearless. She was clothed in silks and velvet, though secondhand of course. Her white charges frequently taught her to read and write. If she did not sleep in the room with the white children, she lived with her husband and family in a cabin, finer than that of the other slaves and close to the "big house." She had no real home life of her own, however, until she became too old to care for her master's children. She and her children were usually safe from sale and corporal punishment. In a large house, she might have younger assistants or "nurses" to care for the children. The mammy was usually the daughter of a previous mammy and grew up as a playmate of the whites. As she grew older, she took on maid's duties and gradually moved into the highest position among the servants. The mammy was wet nurse for the mistress's children, so that the mistress could "get back into shape" as soon as possible; though this duty deprived her own offspring of necessary subsistence. . . .

Many of her charges cared more for her than for their natural mother. She taught them etiquette, position in the plantation hierarchy, and proper respect for different individuals they might encounter. She was permitted to discipline the young white children for transgressions. As the children grew older, she was their confidant in love affairs and was often consulted in their choice of a mate. Mammy was present at her "children's" weddings. To her mistress, she was the oldest, dearest, closest friend. When she passed on to her final reward, she was buried in a proper coffin in the white family's plot with a marker, and the master conducted the burial service. Her husband was usually the butler, driver, gardener, mechanic, or foreman. He might belong to another master, but his conjugal visits came more easily. Overall, the house slaves did not produce wealth. Instead, they represented a draw on the family's finances in the name of prestige and social position.

The field hand produced the wealth that supported the system. The small planter with five or six slaves worked in the field with them as their overseer, while the large planter hired a white overseer to assume responsibility for production. In addition, many colonies had laws requiring a specific proportion of whites to blacks, in order to suppress the constant danger of slave insurrection. A small Southern farmer could not compete with slave labor and frequently lost his farm. All of his instincts should have made him an opponent of slavery. However, he was bombarded by propaganda from the church, newspapers, and political leaders about the benefits of slavery. Negroes were his biological inferiors and could go on a murderous rampage if they were set free. Because the poor white was superior to the slave, he could always aspire to own one or several slaves and join the upper class. It was this landless group that produced the overseer. According to Patrick Henry, he was the most "abject, degraded, unprincipalled [sic] man." The cruelty of the overseer was indirectly caused by his employer, because the hired man had to bring in an adequate crop to keep his job. He signed a contract each year that listed his salary and supplied a house, an allowance of food, and a slave servant. His duties were listed in the contract and included the care and control of the slaves; the amount and kind of labor performed; care of tools and livestock; and his social behavior. He kept daily records of all plantation activities and reported to the owner at specific periods. He assigned the work to the slaves; policed and inspected their quarters to search for weapons; treated sick slaves; punished malingerers and rebellious blacks; and prevented sabotage and stealing. Most overseers remained on a plantation for just two or three years because they rarely met the production demands of the owner. The overseer's life was little better than that of the slaves he controlled. He could not fraternize with the slaves, and his employer's family considered him socially inferior. He could not entertain guests or leave the plantation without permission. Like the slave, he had to hunt, fish, and grow crops to supplement his food ration. His food was similar to that of the slaves in kind and preparation. His "genetic superiority" sustained him through a very unhappy life.

Below the overseer was the driver or foreman. He was a slave hated by the other field hands. The driver supervised his charges minutely. He was usually the strongest slave on the plantation, with a presumed judgment capacity above that of the ordinary slave. His job was a lifetime occupation. In addition to supervising the work of the others, he watched the other slaves' deportment in and out of the fields. He reported daily to the overseer and received his tasks for the following day. In return for his work, he received more food and better clothes. The driver had little free time after work, so the owner compensated him by having other slaves work his plot of land.

The workday could last from dawn to dusk, with two short periods free for food and rest. During the harvest, the work day could last 14–18 hours. To prevent the overseer from pushing his charges beyond human endurance, several colonial legislatures passed laws regulating their work. A law in South Carolina of

1740 stated, "Whereas many owners of slaves, and others who have the care, management, and overseeing of slaves, do confine them so closely to hard labor that they have not sufficient time for natural rest, Be it therefore enacted, that if any owner of slaves, or other persons, who shall have the care, management or overseeing of slaves, shall work or put such slave or slaves to labor more than 15 hours in 24 hours . . . every such person shall forfeit a sum not exceeding £20 nor under £5 current money, for every time he, she, or they shall offend." The law was on the books, but its enforcement was questionable.

A Visitor Describes the Colonies

Andrew Burnaby

Reverend Andrew Burnaby, one of a growing number of Europeans intrigued by the prospects, ambitions, and attitudes of the American colonies, made several expeditions into the American countryside during the 1760s. He recorded his observations of the continent in a collection of travel notes for his European audience, in which he expresses ambivalence toward the quality of American life. Although he sees potential and beauty in these new lands, Burnaby also concludes that the colonies could not rule themselves and have tremendous obstacles to overcome before they can stand strong and united.

From what has been said of this colony [Virginia], it will not be difficult to form an idea of the character of its inhabitants. The climate and external appearance of the country conspire to make them indolent, easy, and good natured; extremely fond of society, and much given to convivial pleasures. In consequence of this, they seldom show any spirit of enterprise, or expose themselves willingly to fatigue. Their authority over their slaves renders them vain and imperious, and entire strangers to that elegance of sentiment, which is so peculiarly characteristic of refined and polished nations. Their ignorance of mankind and of learning, exposes them to many errors and prejudices, especially in regard to Indians and negroes, whom they scarcely consider as of the human species; so that it is almost impossible, in cases of violence, or even murder, committed upon those unhappy people by any of the planters, to have the delinquents brought to justice: for either the grand jury refuse to find the bill, or the petit jury bring in their verdict, not guilty.

The display of a character thus constituted, will naturally be in acts of extravagance, ostentation, and a disregard of economy; it

Andrew Burnaby, *Andrew Burnaby's Travels Through North America, 1759–1760.* New York: Andrew Burnaby, 1904.

is not extraordinary therefore, that the Virginians outrun their incomes; and that having involved themselves in difficulties, they are frequently tempted to raise money by bills of exchange, which they know will be returned protested, with 10 percent interest.

The public or political character of the Virginians corresponds with their private one: they are haughty and jealous of their liberties, impatient of restraint, and can scarcely bear the thought of being controlled by any superior power. Many of them consider the colonies as independent states, not connected with Great Britain, otherwise than by having the same common king, and being bound to her by natural affection. There are but few of them that have a turn for business, and even those are by no means expert at it. I have known them, upon a very urgent occasion, vote the relief of a garrison, without once considering whether the thing was practicable, when it was most evidently and demonstrably otherwise. In matters of commerce they are ignorant of the necessary principles that must prevail between a colony and the mother country; they think it a hardship not to have an unlimited trade to every part of the world. They consider the duties upon their staple as injurious only to themselves; and it is utterly impossible to persuade them that they affect the consumer also. However, to do them justice, the same spirit of generosity prevails here which does in their private character; they never refuse any necessary supplies for the support of government when called upon, and are a generous and loyal people.

The women are, generally speaking, handsome, though not to be compared with our fair countrywomen in England. They have but few advantages, and consequently are seldom accomplished; this makes them reserved, and unequal to any interesting or refined conversation. They are immoderately fond of dancing, and indeed it is almost the only amusement they partake of: but even in this they discover want of taste and elegance, and seldom appear with that gracefulness and ease, which these movements are calculated to display. Towards the close of an evening, when the company are pretty well tired with country dances, it is usual to dance jigs; a practice originally borrowed, I am informed, from the negroes. These dances are without method or regularity: a gentleman and lady stand up, and dance about the room, one of them retiring, the other pursuing, then perhaps meeting, in an irregular fantastical manner. After some time, another lady gets up, and then the first lady must sit down, she being, as they term it, cut out: the second lady acts the same part which the first did, till somebody cuts her out. The gentlemen perform in the same manner. The Virginian ladies, excepting these amusements, and now and then going upon a party of pleasure into the woods to partake of a barbecue, chiefly spend their time in sewing and taking care of their families: they seldom read, or endeavour to improve their minds; however, they are in general good housewives; and though they have not, I think, quite so much tenderness and sensibility as the English ladies, yet they make as good wives, and as good mothers, as any in the world.

The Possibilities for Prosperity and the Example of Pennsylvania

It is hard to determine whether this colony can be called flourishing, or not; because though it produces great quantities of tobacco and grain, yet there seem to be very few improvements carrying on in it. Great part of Virginia is a wilderness, and as many of the gentlemen are in possession of immense tracts of land, it is likely to continue so. A spirit of enterprise is by no means the turn of the colony, and therefore few attempts have been made to force a trade; which I think might easily be done, both to the West Indies and the Ohio. They have every thing necessary for such an undertaking; viz. lumber, provisions, grain, and every other commodity, which the other colonies, that subsist and grow rich by these means, make use of for exports; but, instead of this, they have only a trifling communication with the West Indies; and as to the Ohio, they have suffered themselves, notwithstanding the superior advantages they might enjoy from having a water carriage almost to the Youghiogheny, to neglect this valuable branch of commerce; while the industrious Pennsylvanians seize every opportunity, and struggle with innumerable difficulties to secure it to themselves. The Virginians are content if they can but live from day to day; they confine themselves almost entirely to the cultivation of tobacco; and if they have but enough of this to pay their merchants in London, and to provide for their pleasures, they are satisfied, and desire nothing more.

Some few, indeed, have been rather more enterprising, and have endeavoured to improve their estates by raising indigo, and other schemes: but whether it has been owing to the climate, to their inexperience in these matters, or their want of perseverance, I am unable to determine. . . .

Can the mind have a greater pleasure than in contemplating the rise and progress of cities and kingdoms? Than in perceiving a rich and opulent state arising out of a small settlement or colony? This pleasure every one must feel who considers Pennsylvania. This wonderful province is situated between the 40th and 43d degree of north latitude, and about 76 degrees west longitude from London, in a healthy and delightful climate, amidst all the advantages that nature can bestow. The soil is extremely strong and fertile, and produces spontaneously an infinite variety of trees, flowers, fruits, and plants of different sorts. The mountains are enriched with ore, and the rivers with fish: some of these are so stately as not to be beheld without admiration: the Delaware is navigable for large vessels as far as the falls, 180 miles distant from the sea, and 120 from the bay. At the mouth it is more than three miles broad, and above one at Philadelphia. The navigation is obstructed in the winter, for about six weeks, by the severity of the frost; but, at other times, it is bold and open. The Schuylkill, though not navigable for any great space, is exceedingly romantic, and affords the most delightful retirements.

The Growth of Pennsylvania Industry

Cultivation (comparatively speaking) is carried to a high degree of perfection; and Pennsylvania produces not only great plenty, but also great variety of grain; it yields likewise flax-seed, hemp, cattle of different kinds, and various other articles.

It is divided into eight counties, and contains many large and populous towns: Carlisle, Lancaster, and Germantown, consist each of near five hundred houses; there are several others which have from one or two hundred.

The number of inhabitants is supposed to be between four and five hundred thousand, a fifth of which are Quakers; there are very few negroes or slaves.

The trade of Pennsylvania is surprisingly extensive, carried on to Great Britain, the West Indies, every part of North America, the Madeiras, Lisbon, Cadiz, Holland, Africa, the Spanish Main, and several other places; exclusive of what is illicitly carried on to Cape François, and Monte Christo. Their exports are provisions of all kinds, lumber, hemp, flax, flax-seed, iron, furs, and deer-skins. Their imports, English manufactures, with the superfluities and luxuries of life. By their flag-of-truce trade, they also get sugar, which they refine and send to Europe.

Their manufactures are very considerable. The Germantown thread-stockings are in high estimation; and the year before last, I have been credibly informed, there were manufactured in that town alone above 60,000 dozen pair. Their common retail price is a dollar per pair.

The Irish settlers make very good linens: some woolens have also been fabricated, but not, I believe, to any amount. There are several other manufactures, viz. of beaver hats, which are superior in goodness to any in Europe, of cordage, linseed-oil, starch, myrtle-wax and spermaceti candles, soap, earthen ware, and other commodities.

Institutional Developments

The government of this province is a proprietary one. The legislature is lodged in the hands of a governor, appointed (with the king's approbation) by the proprietor; and a house of representatives elected by the people, consisting of thirty-seven members. These are of various religious persuasions; for by the charter of privileges which Mr. [William] Penn granted to the settlers in Pennsylvania, no person who believed in God could be molested in his calling or profession; and any one who believed in Jesus Christ might enjoy the first post under the government. The crown has reserved to itself a power of repealing any law, which may interfere with the prerogative, or be contrary to the laws of Great Britain. . . .

As to religion, there is none properly established; but Protestants of all denominations, Papists, Jews, and all other sects whatsoever, are universally tolerated. There are twelve clergymen of the Church of England, who are sent by the Society for the Propagation of the Gospel, and are allowed annually 50 l. [pounds] each, besides what they get from subscriptions and surplice fees. Some few of these are itinerant missionaries, and have no fixed residence, but travel from place to place, as occasion requires, upon the frontiers. They are under the jurisdiction of the bishop of London.

Arts and sciences are yet in their infancy. There are some few persons who have discovered a taste for music and painting; and philosophy seems not only to have made a considerable progress already, but to be daily gaining ground. The library society is an excellent institution for propagating a taste for literature; and the college well calculated to form and cultivate it. This last institution is erected upon an admirable plan, and is by far the best school for learning throughout America. It has been chiefly raised by contributions; and its present fund is about 10,000 l. Pennsylvania money. An account of it may be seen in Dr. Smith's (the president's) Discourses. The Quakers also have an academy for instructing their youth in classical learning, and practical mathematics: there are three teachers, and about seventy boys in it. Besides these, there are several schools in the province for the Dutch and other foreign children; and a considerable one is going to be erected at Germantown.

The People of Pennsylvania

The Pennsylvanians, as to character, are a frugal and industrious people: not remarkably courteous and hospitable to strangers, unless particularly recommended to them; but rather, like the denizens of most commercial cities, the reverse. They are great republicans, and have fallen into the same errors in their ideas of independency as most of the other colonies have. They are by far the most enterprising people upon the continent. As they consist of several nations, and talk several languages, they are aliens in some respect to Great Britain: nor can it be expected that they should have the same filial attachment to her which her own immediate offspring have. However, they are quiet, and concern themselves but little, except about getting money. The women are exceedingly handsome and polite; they are naturally sprightly and fond of pleasure; and, upon the whole, are much more agreeable and accomplished than the men. Since their intercourse with the English officers, they are greatly improved; and, without flattery, many of them would not make bad figures even in the first assemblies in Europe. Their amusements are chiefly, dancing in the winter; and, in the summer, forming parties of pleasure upon the Schuylkill, and in the country. There is a society of sixteen ladies, and as many gentlemen, called the fishing company, who meet once a fortnight upon the Schuylkill. They have a very pleasant room erected in a romantic situation upon the banks of that river, where they generally dine and drink tea. There are several pretty walks about it, and some wild and rugged rocks, which, together with the water and free groves that adorn the banks, form a most beautiful and picturesque scene. There are boats and fishing tackle of all sorts, and the company divert themselves with walking, fishing, going up the water, dancing, singing, conversing, or just as they please. The ladies wear an uniform, and appear with great ease and advantage from the neatness and simplicity of it. The first and most distinguished people of the colony are of this society; and it is very advantageous to a stranger to be introduced to it, as he hereby gets acquainted with the best and most respectable company in Philadelphia. In the winter, when there is snow upon the ground, it is usual to make what they call sleighing parties, or to go upon it in sledges; but as this is a practice well known in Europe, it is needless to describe it. . . .

A Final Assessment of the Colonies

Having travelled over so large a tract of this vast continent, before I bid a final farewell to it, I must beg the reader's indulgence, while I stop for a moment, and as it were from the top of a high eminence, take one general retrospective look at the whole. An idea, strange as it is visionary, has entered into the minds of the generality of mankind, that empire is travelling westward; and every one is looking forward with eager and impatient expectation to that destined moment when America is to give law to the rest of the world. But if ever an idea was illusory and fallacious, I am fully persuaded, that this will be so.

America is formed for happiness, but not for empire: in a course of 1,200 miles I did not see a single object that solicited charity; but I saw insuperable causes of weakness, which will necessarily prevent its being a potent state.

Our colonies may be distinguished into the southern and northern, separated from each other by the Susquehanna and that imaginary line which divides Maryland from Pennsylvania.

The southern colonies have so many inherent causes of weakness, that they never can possess any real strength. The climate operates very powerfully upon them, and renders them indolent, inactive, and unenterprising; this is visible in every line of their character. I myself have been a spectator, and it is not an uncommon sight, of a man in the vigour of life, lying upon a couch, and a female slave standing over him, wafting off the flies, and fanning him, while he took his repose.

The southern colonies (Maryland, which is the smallest and most inconsiderable, alone excepted) will never be thickly seated: for as they are not confined within determinate limits, but extend to the westward indefinitely, men, sooner than apply to laborious occupations, occupations militating with their dispositions, and generally considered too as the inheritance and badge of slavery, will gradually retire westward, and settle upon fresh lands, which are said also to be more fertile; where, by the servitude of a negro or two, they may enjoy all the satisfaction of an easy and indolent independency: hence the lands upon the coast will of course remain thin of inhabitants.

The mode of cultivation by slavery, is another insurmountable cause of weakness. The number of negroes in the southern colonies is upon the whole nearly equal, if not superior, to that of the white men; and they propagate and increase even faster. Their condition is truly pitiable; their labour excessively hard, their diet poor and scanty, their treatment cruel and oppressive: they cannot therefore but be a subject of terror to those who so inhumanly tyrannize over them.

The Indians near the frontiers are a still further formidable cause of subjection. The southern Indians are numerous, and are governed by a sounder policy than formerly: experience has taught them wisdom. They never make war with the colonists without carrying terror and devastation along with them. They sometimes break up entire counties together. Such is the state of the southern colonies.

The northern colonies are of stronger stamina, but they have other difficulties and disadvantages to struggle with, not less arduous, or more easy to be surmounted, than what have been already mentioned. Their limits being defined, they will undoubtedly become exceedingly populous: for though men will readily retire back towards the frontiers of their own colony, yet they will not so easily be induced to settle beyond them, where different laws and polities prevail; and where, in short, they are a different people: but in proportion to want of territory, if we consider the proposition in a general and abstract light, will be want of power. But the northern colonies have still more positive and real disadvantages to contend with. They are composed of people of different nations, different manners, different religions, and different languages. They have a mutual jealousy of each other, fomented by considerations of interest, power, and ascendancy. Religious zeal, too, like a smothered fire, is secretly burning in the hearts of the different sectaries that inhabit them, and were it not restrained by laws and superior authority, would soon burst out into a flame of universal persecution. Even the peaceable Quakers struggle hard for preeminence, and evince in a very striking manner that the passions of mankind are much stronger than any principles of religion.

Despite Their Progress, the Colonies Remain Isolated and Weak

The colonies, therefore, separately considered, are internally weak; but it may be supposed, that, by an union or coalition, they would become strong and formidable: but an union seems almost impossible: one founded in dominion or power is morally so: for, were not England to interfere, the colonies themselves so well understand the policy of preserving a balance, that, I think, they would not be idle spectators, were any one of them to endeavour to subjugate its next neighbour. Indeed, it appears to me a very doubtful point, even supposing all the colonies of America to be united under one head, whether it would be possible to keep in due order and government so wide and extended an empire, the difficulties of communication, of intercourse, of correspondence, and all other circumstances considered.

A voluntary association or coalition, at least a permanent one, is almost as difficult to be supposed: for fire and water are not more heterogeneous than the different colonies in North America. Nothing can exceed the jealousy and emulation which they possess in regard to each other. The inhabitants of Pennsylvania and New York have an inexhaustible source of animosity, in their jealousy for the trade of the Jerseys. Massachusetts Bay and Rhode Island, are not less interested in that of Connecticut. The West Indies are a common subject of emulation to them all. Even the limits and boundaries of each colony are a constant source of litigation. In short, such is the difference of character, of manners, of religion, of interest, of the different colonies, that I think, if I am not wholly ignorant of the human mind, were they left to themselves, there would soon be a civil war from one end of the continent to the other; while the Indians and negroes would, with better reason, impatiently watch the opportunity of exterminating them all together.

Religion and Education in the Colonies

CHAPTER
2

Chapter Preface

Once the colonial settlers had established their communities and churches, they turned their attention to schooling. Education for boys—girls were not allowed to attend school whatsoever in colonial America—was an essential part of the colonists' dream for America. Each settlement went about teaching the youth in a different manner. In the southern and middle colonies, learning took place at home or in private institutions. There were no formal schoolhouses in the southern colonies; if parents wanted their children educated outside of the home, they sent them away to schools in England. The middle colonies had authoritarian schools that taught practical subjects such as surveying, reading, and writing as well as Bible studies. Public education first started in Puritan New England and was closely aligned and in tune with Puritan religious beliefs. In the northern and middle colonies, the schoolmaster and parents expected children to study hard, memorize their catechisms, and obey and respect their elders. The pedagogies used to teach them reinforced these ideas.

The first schools were strict, cold, and authoritarian. The teachers often beat and humiliated students in front of their peers, and the lessons were difficult and dogmatic. Students were encouraged to memorize their lessons and could not ask for help for fear of being harshly persecuted. They sat on backless benches for up to eight hours a day. And parents, especially in Puritan New England, approved of the harsh discipline, believing that if a schoolboy was not being whipped often, he must not be learning much. Throughout the colonies, schooling was seen to aid in moral and social instruction. Much of the reading instruction in the colonies was given so that people could read the Bible. This was the primary reason for literacy in the colonies, and ambitious parents often taught their children to read the Bible when they were toddlers. The reading primers that were assigned often taught Puritan doctrines in simplistic ways that could be understood by their readers.

The strong religious beliefs of the colonists greatly influenced the ways in which they taught their children and the public school system that they created. From the informal learning that took place in their homes to the formal schools used to instill a strong moral character and piety in the students, colonial systems of education worked to advance cultural knowledge and intelligence in a new land. Much of the learning necessary to living and surviving in the new, unsettled frontier territories was passed down from parents to children. Skills such as hunting, fishing, cooking, making clothing, and developing sustainable agricultures, though not taught in formal settings, were instrumental in the colonists' survival.

Religion and Education

Richard Middleton

Richard Middleton, senior professor in American history at Queens University in Belfast, explains that religion was a fundamental aspect of civilization in all of the colonies. According to Middleton, who has taught in both the British Isles and the United States, the religious revival known as the Great Awakening significantly affected the many creeds that established themselves in America, from Puritan to Quaker to Protestant. The religious beliefs of the colonists informed their views of education and higher learning, leading to the establishment of the first universities in America. However, with the rise of scientific reasoning during the second half of the eighteenth century, the colleges moved away from strict institutions of religious instruction and began to focus on the pursuit of scientific and artistic knowledge.

E xcept for work, religion remained the most important aspect of colonial life, even in the South. Although the fires of religious conviction perhaps burned less fiercely after 1689, religion was still a crucial element in people's lives, particularly in their limited periods of relaxation.

Religion retained its hold for a number of reasons. It provided the community with a sense of purpose; it was a socially desirable habit; it still provided the best explanation of the world; and it gave people the hope of an afterlife. When existence was so harsh and its duration so uncertain, religion offered at least some comfort to most people. Not that salvation was easy; God was still seen as a vengeful deity who punished the wicked by sending them to hell. Only a minority would go to heaven.

Nevertheless, important developments had taken place. In New England the need to expand the elect had led some ministers to extend the communion. The first tentative steps in this direction had been taken by Thomas Hooker in seventeenth-century Connecticut. Toward the end of his ministry, Hooker had opened communion at Hartford to all adults of good behavior, believing that only God could judge whether someone was of the elect. At the same time he urged everyone to prepare for salvation. Hooker argued that God had not necessarily made up his mind about every individual. Grace might still be achieved if the covenant were observed.

Hooker's ideas were later adopted at Northampton, further up the Connecticut Valley, where Solomon Stoddard was the minister. Opponents like Cotton Mather understandably argued that Hooker and Stoddard were preaching a covenant of works. Nevertheless, Stoddard was not prevented from continuing these practices when the Massachusetts synod of ministers was convened in 1679. Increasingly others followed his lead, notably the Brattle Street Church in Boston. After 1700 most churches began offering communion to all who appeared of a godly disposition, effectively ending the distinction between the elect and the rest of the congregation. . . .

Change in the Churches

Although religion remained the single most important activity outside work, all the churches believed that their flock were sinking into irreligion and godlessness. . . .

Historians now believe that no serious declension in religious belief was taking place. Nevertheless, attempts continued to be made to enhance the appeal of the churches by relaxing membership requirements and adopting a more rational approach. Paradoxically these attempts at modernization were to cost the major churches dear. As sermons became ever more theoretical and philosophical in content, they provided opportunities for the Baptists to pick up converts from denominations which had lost their fire. The Baptists had first arrived in the 1650s, preaching the need for adult baptism and attacking the idea of state-supported churches. Their simple style won them many converts, especially in the South, where their ministers courageously journeyed to the farthest habitations. By the late colonial period they had perhaps three hundred congregations.

The most persuasive challenge to the major churches came

from the phenomenon known as the Great Awakening, which began in a number of different places as individual ministers sought to revive religious feeling through evangelical methods. Their efforts involved placing greater emphasis on the four gospels with their message of glad tidings and salvation. One of the first to adopt this method was Theodore Frelinghuysen of the Dutch Reformed church in the Raritan Valley in 1726. His success in rousing his congregation was emulated by other ministers, notably the venerable Solomon Stoddard, who was still seeking to re-create the first church of Christ at Northampton, Massachusetts. In New Jersey the evangelical style of preaching was first adopted by the Presbyterian Gilbert Tennent and his son William, a close associate of Frelinghuysen.

The movement's most important boost came with the arrival of George Whitefield, one of the founders of Methodism. Methodists were generally Anglicans who, like many denominations, found that their church had lost its vitality in the face of abstract theology and the defense of established privileges. They preached a new evangelical message that all men could be saved if they turned to God. In some respects the Great Awakening was a return to the old belief in salvation through faith and God's saving grace. Since the turn of the century most churches had veered implicitly toward a brand of Arminianism which was linked to the concept of free will and the belief that humanity could save itself.

All this the Great Awakening rejected, seeking instead to center religion once more on the heart rather than the head, on faith rather than reason, and on grace rather than good works. Even more important than its theology was the movement's style; its proponents reached out to the mass of the population by preaching in fields in what became the first mass revivals of modern times.

Whitefield himself came to America in 1739 on the first of seven tours. Beginning in Savannah, he proceeded up the coast to Philadelphia before returning via the backcountry to Charleston. In August 1740 he traveled to New England, after drawing crowds of many thousands all along his route. In Philadelphia he impressed even the cynical [Ben] Franklin with the power of his delivery, the simpleness of his message, and his ability to be heard.

Whitefield's greatest triumphs, however, came in New England, where his itinerant style of preaching was as yet hardly permitted. When pulpits were denied him, he took to the fields, followed by huge crowds. Everywhere he subjected his listeners to the certainty of hellfire and eternal damnation unless repentance was immediate and complete. Thousands wept for their sins.

The Movement Challenges Traditions

Whitefield and his imitators posed a serious challenge to the established churches. The speed of their conversions and indifference to denominational boundaries inevitably caused dispute. Many ministers, recognizing the revivalists' appeal, opened their doors in the belief that their techniques would help rekindle the religious zeal of their own congregations. Others, notably Charles Chauncey of Boston's First Church, rejected this approach, feeling that such enthusiasm was of little value in awakening real spirituality and that only a proper appreciation of Christ could bring an individual real grace.

The result was an internal split in many churches, notably among the Presbyterians of the middle colonies and the Congregationalists of New England, where both denominations established rival congregations in many towns. Among the Presbyterians divisions were especially bitter after Gilbert Tennent published his pamphlet *The Danger of an Unconverted Ministry*, which attacked the conservatives. The two groups came to be known as the New and Old Lights representing the radical and conservative wings respectively. Some of these rifts healed after a few years; others remained. Many New Lights subsequently found that the Baptist church met their desire for a more informal, less institutionalized religion. . . .

One important, though unintended, consequence of the Great Awakening was the advancement of toleration, for even New Englanders recognized that uniformity was an ideal which could no longer be attained. In other respects the movement's effects seem to have been limited. Within a few months of Whitefield's preaching, the population began to lose its enthusiasm. Soon the ministers were warning once more of the failings of their flock. The most insidious threat to the godly kingdom was that of materialism, the constant desire for "improving and advancing."

One sign of this trend was the increasingly female composition of congregations as men turned their attentions to other pursuits. The danger seemed most obvious in the larger towns, where churchgoing was in decline.

Whatever the complaints of the ministers, the colonists remained overtly religious in their attitudes and culture. Most attended church on Sunday to listen to sermons of an hour or more. Concern for religion continued to dominate the thoughts of legislators and the governing classes. Most colonies retained laws like Virginia's 1691 act for the "more Effectual Suppressing of Swearing, Cursing, Profaning God's Holy Name, Sabbath Abusing, Drunkeness, Fornication, and Adultery." The desire was still to effect a godly society, even if the laws were breached increasingly in both letter and spirit.

Religious Education: Puritan Schooling

America has a long tradition of providing free schooling for its citizens and was the first nation to do so. The origins of this achievement can be traced back to the colonial period.

We have seen that the first educational establishments, notably those in New England, were motivated by religious considerations. Persons wishing to be saved must be conversant with the word of God and therefore required the ability to read the Bible. Another consideration was the need for a trained ministry.

To these ends schools and colleges were established from an early stage in New England. A Massachusetts Law of 1647, the first regulating education, stated that if parents neglected to instruct their children, the selectmen could apprentice them so that they could "read and understand the principles of religion and the capital laws of the country." Connecticut passed a similar law in 1650.

In smaller communities most instruction was provided in "dame" schools, where the teacher was a female member of the church. Only the larger towns could afford a qualified master to run a grammar school, and these were restricted to boys. Nevertheless, by 1700 some 70 percent of men and 45 percent of women could read and write. The figures continued to climb throughout the colonial period as communities became more settled, but literacy remained essentially a religious rather than a

secular quest. Its value in advancing a person's skills and liveli-
hood was not generally accepted until after the Revolution.

Education in the Middle and Southern States

Outside New England, schooling was more haphazard, on account of different attitudes among the other churches. Most left
the attainment of salvation to guidance by the minister rather
than personal study by the individual. Such elitist views were especially prevalent in the Anglican church. The rector's sermons,
services, and parish visits were thought to be sufficient guidance
for the congregation, though education was seen as a legitimate
part of the missionary process. The least concerned with education were the Baptists and Quakers, who relied on inspiration
and spontaneity, for which neither formal training nor literacy
was necessary.

In the middle and southern colonies schooling was accordingly
left to individual parishes and communities. Large towns like
New York and Philadelphia had schools by the end of the seventeenth century, though the emphasis remained religious. The
first school in New York was established by the Dutch Reformed
church, followed in 1710 by Trinity School. . . . In Philadelphia
the first educational institution was the Friends' School, founded
by the Quakers in 1689. Elsewhere, especially in the South, the
only instruction available was by private tutor, though many parents did their best to pass on their skills.

As the eighteenth century progressed, the need for better
schools was recognized not just by the churches. This increased
awareness in part reflected a growing need for clerks and other
literate persons in commerce, law, and administration. The
growth of education was also a response to the Enlightenment,
as the more affluent began to sense that they could improve
themselves materially as well as morally if they were educated.

These factors resulted in greater efforts to provide schooling.
In Maryland attempts were made in 1723 to set up county
schools for the poor, while in the Charleston area a number of
"free" schools were established where only the better off had to
pay. This increase in schools in turn led more people to contem-
plate a career in teaching, which had now become accepted as a

separate vocation from the ministry, though many people continued to practice both. Another aid to educational expansion was an increase in the number of legacies left to schools. The consequence was a respectable increase in literacy even in Virginia, where perhaps two-thirds of males could read documents and sign their names by 1760. Pennsylvania had roughly the same literacy level.

The figure for women's literacy is less definite, but it was certainly lower, perhaps only half that of males. Since women could not be ministers or participate in public life, the benefits of educating them were less apparent. An ability to read was all that was required except for the daughters of the elite, who required additional social graces.

Establishing Universities

We have already seen that New England was also at the forefront of higher education with the founding of Harvard in 1636 to provide a trained ministry. The college was never intended solely as a seminary, for in addition to theological topics, instruction was offered in "good literature, arts and sciences." Nevertheless, until the end of the colonial period any male wishing to graduate in anything other than classics, divinity, and philosophy had to journey across the Atlantic for his education. The most popular subjects were medicine in Edinburgh and law in London.

Harvard remained the only institution of higher learning in America for fifty years until the College of William and Mary was established at Williamsburg in 1693 as a belated response by the Anglican community there to the need for a trained ministry. The lack of a higher institution to prepare Anglican clergy had hampered the Episcopalian cause, although with no bishop in America, candidates still had to cross the Atlantic to be ordained. The first president and founding father was a Scottish Episcopalian, James Blair, who always intended William and Mary to be a college as well as a seminary to cater for the needs of the Virginian planters.

Blair's friendship with [philosopher] John Locke was reflected in the college's curriculum, which provided for the study of medicine and law in addition to the more traditional classics and theology. In 1717 the first chair in natural philosophy and mathematics was created. But though generously endowed, the college languished because of internal squabbles. A serious fire also destroyed most of the main building in 1705. As a result some planters continued to send their sons to England for their education, especially in law.

By the turn of the eighteenth century, Harvard had begun to adopt more liberal attitudes in religious matters, reflecting the growth of Arminian views. Not everyone welcomed this trend, and as a result Yale was founded in 1701 to produce ministers of a more orthodox stance. The curriculum at the new college was similar to that of Harvard in the previous century, having a heavy emphasis on classics, divinity, and philosophy. In due course Yale, too, found that it could not divorce itself from the intellectual currents which were sweeping Europe. By 1760 it was little different from its rival.

Colleges in the Middle Colonies

The middle colonies had to wait longer for an institution of higher learning. New York lacked a single dominant religious group, while Quaker Pennsylvania felt no need of one, having no trained ministry. The Quakers in any case laid more emphasis on the "university of life", as Benjamin Franklin termed it. However, as the Presbyterians grew in strength, they became increasingly eager to have some institution to train their ministers. A few candidates attended Harvard, and in 1726 William Tennent established a "log college" at Neshaminy in Bucks County, Pennsylvania, though the project was underfunded and did not survive. In 1746 a group of New Light Scottish Presbyterians in Elizabethtown founded the College of New Jersey, which later merged with another small academy at Newark. In 1754 new premises were established at Princeton, though the college was not known by that name until the 1760s. From the beginning it was interdenominational; indeed, its third president was Jonathan Edwards. And like Harvard, Yale, and William and Mary, Princeton had many students who were not candidates for the ministry.

Meanwhile, under Benjamin Franklin's guidance, in 1751 the Academy of Philadelphia had been founded, with the distinction of being the first secular institution to impose no religious test for admission. Its aim was to increase knowledge as an end in itself. As Franklin argued in his initial appeal, this was the surest way to advance "the happiness both of private families and of commonwealths." Franklin was heavily influenced by his Quaker surroundings and by the educational philosophy of Locke. The academy therefore placed a heavy emphasis on what was useful. Among the proposed subjects were arithmetic, accounts, geometry, and astronomy. Also included were English and history, to show "the beauty and usefulness of virtue"; natural history and botany, to contribute to the "improvement of agriculture"; and mechanics, "by which weak men perform such wonders, labour is saved, manufactures expedited." The academy also taught Greek and Latin, which were useful in the study of divinity, law, medicine, and modern languages.

Lastly, in 1754 New York obtained its first institution of higher learning with the establishment of King's College. The Anglicans had tried to charter a college in 1746 but had been prevented by the Presbyterians in the assembly, where neither group was sufficiently dominant to dictate its wishes. When King's College finally opened, therefore, it was effectively a nondenominational institution. Its curriculum was centered on "the learned languages" and "liberal arts and sciences." Entrants had to be able to read and write, have basic arithmetic, and possess a good knowledge of Greek and Latin.

By 1760, then, six colonies had institutions of higher learning, five of them in the north. This distribution reflected the concentration of dissenting churches there rather than a northern commitment to education itself, though urbanization may also have been a factor. All were exclusively male. An increasing number of students no longer intended to be ministers, however, having more secular ends in view. For a growing segment of society, saving the world was no longer a primary aim. But although all the colleges were broadening their curriculum by 1760, they still only partially met the needs of professions like law and medicine. Until the Revolution, those who could not afford to study in Europe had to graduate from a colonial college and then practice with someone already qualified in the profession. . . .

With the advent of the eighteenth century, colonists in the more settled areas were becoming more affluent and, as a result, eager to acquire the better things in life. They therefore bought English books or copied London furniture styles. This inclination was natural. England was a land of five million people in 1700, where America still contained barely three hundred thousand. The mother country had a sophistication which the colonists wanted to imitate. . . .

On the other hand, while looking instinctively to England to replenish their cultural roots, many colonists were third- or fourth-generation settlers. They spoke American English and had a distinct accent. Increasingly they sent their offspring to local academies, modeled on English institutions but inevitably distinctive in what they taught. The virtues of a colonial education were first expressed when students at the College of William and Mary asserted, at a May Day address in 1699, that a Virginian education was to be preferred even to one in England. This sentiment might have been an overstatement at the time, but it was a portent of things to come.

Religious Fervor: Puritan New England

Alan Taylor

Historian and professor Alan Taylor's interest in the diversity of early American history is reflected in this excerpt from his 2001 book, *American Colonies*. In the following selection, Taylor details the lives, beliefs, and obsessively moralistic pursuits of the Puritan colonialists. The industry, relative equality, education, and sense of morals that they embraced left an "enduring Puritan legacy in English-speaking America." Nevertheless, Taylor also acknowledges the downfalls and problems associated with the Puritan New Englanders' missionary zeal and repressive religiosity.

B egun as an epithet, "Puritan" persists in scholarship to name the broad movement of diverse people who shared a conviction that the Protestant Reformation remained incomplete in England. Because the monarchs favored religious compromise and inclusion, the Anglican Church was, in the horrified words of one Puritan, "a mingle-mangle" of Protestant and Catholic doctrines and ceremonies. The ecclesiastical structure of bishops and archbishops remained Catholic except for the substitution at the top of the king for the pope.

In seeking reform, Puritans divided over the details. Most remained within the Anglican Church, seeking to capture and reform it, preserving the link between church and state. The more radical Puritans, however, became "Separatists," determined immediately to withdraw into their own independent congregations. Without any larger authority to enforce orthodoxy, the many autonomous Separatist congregations steadily splintered in their beliefs and practices, forming many distinct sects.

Disdaining the legacy of medieval Catholicism, the Puritans sought to recover the original, pure, and simple church of Jesus

Christ and his apostles. In a "Reformed Church" individual souls could nurture a more direct relationship with God. Rejecting the intercession of priests administering ceremonial sacraments, the Puritans instead urged every believer to seek God by reading the Bible, forming prayer groups, and heeding learned and zealous ministers who delivered evangelical sermons. Puritans wished to strip away church ceremony and formulaic prayers as legacies of papacy. They also wanted to eliminate or reduce the authority of the bishops by increasing the authority of local congregations.

Puritans longed to experience the "New Birth": a transforming infusion of divine grace that liberated people from profound anxiety over their spiritual worthlessness and eternal fate. By moral living, devout prayer, reading the Bible, and heeding sermons, the hopeful Puritan prepared for the possibility of God's saving grace. But not even the most devout could claim conversion and salvation as a right and a certainty, for God alone determined. He saved selectively and arbitrarily, rather than universally or as a reward for good behavior. In this belief in God's complete power over grace and salvation, the Puritans elaborated upon the "Calvinist" doctrines of the sixteenth-century Swiss theologian Jean Calvin. . . .

Troubles Cause Puritans to Immigrate to the New World

During the late 1620s and early 1630s, [bishop William] Laud and most other bishops enforced the new Anglican orthodoxy, dismissing Puritan ministers who balked at conducting the high church liturgy. Church courts also prosecuted growing numbers of Puritan laypeople. Laud strictly censored Puritan tracts and had pilloried, mutilated, and branded three Puritans who illegally published their ideas. Puritan hopes of securing redress dissipated after 1629, when Charles I dissolved Parliament and proceeded to rule arbitrarily for the next eleven years. Faced with the growing power of the king and his bishops, some despairing Puritans considered emigrating across the Atlantic to a New England.

The Puritan emigrants followed French and English mariners, fishermen, and fur traders who had visited the New England coast during the summers. In 1607 English West Country promoters established a small settlement at the mouth of the Kennebec River on the coast of Maine. But Indian hostility and the hard winter demoralized the colonists who eagerly sailed home in the spring of 1608. Their failure saddled the region with a daunting reputation as frigid and hostile. Determined to improve that reputation, Captain John Smith (of Jamestown fame) explored the coast in 1614 and named it New England because, he claimed, the climate and soil replicated the mother country. Smith published promotional literature, including an appealing map, which greatly intrigued Puritans disgruntled with their Anglican rulers.

The first Puritan emigrants consisted of 102 Separatists, subsequently called the Pilgrims. In 1620 they crossed the Atlantic in the ship *Mayflower* to found a town named Plymouth on the south shore of Massachusetts Bay. Beneficiaries of a devastating epidemic that had recently decimated the coastal Indians, the Plymouth colonists occupied an abandoned village with conveniently cleared fields. In 1620–21, a long, hard, starving winter killed half of the newcomers, but thereafter good crops and more emigrants

After a two-month voyage across the Atlantic, the first Pilgrims land at Plymouth in December 1620.

from England stabilized and strengthened the colony. By 1630 about fifteen hundred English dwelled in the Plymouth colony.

In 1630 a much larger Puritan emigration, subsequently called the "Great Migration," began under the leadership of John Winthrop. A genteel lawyer, Winthrop represented a syndicate of wealthy Puritans who obtained a royal charter as the Massachusetts Bay Company. Unlike those of its unfortunate predecessor, the Virginia Company, the leaders of the Massachusetts Bay Company quickly relocated themselves, with their capital, charter, and records, to New England. In effect, they converted their commercial charter into a self-governing colony three thousand miles away from bishops and king. Once in Massachusetts, the company leaders established the most radical government in the European world: a republic, where the Puritan men elected their governor, deputy governor, and legislature (known as the General Court). Until his death in 1649, John Winthrop almost always won annual reelection as governor.

Beginning with a settlement named Boston, Winthrop's Puritans established the Massachusetts Bay colony on the coast north of Plymouth. After a hungry winter in 1630–31, the Massachusetts colonists raised enough food to sustain themselves and numerous new emigrants, who followed throughout the decade. In New England, the starving time of adjustment proved far shorter and less deadly than in the Chesapeake.

From the coastal towns, the colonists expanded into the interior during the 1630s and 1640s. The expansion troubled colonial leaders who preferred consolidated settlement as more secure from Indian attack and more convenient to sustain schools and churches. But the colonists could not resist the allure of spreading out in search of larger tracts of land for farming. And the colonial Puritans were discovering their disagreements over the proper rules to govern their new towns and churches. Often with a push from local majorities, the disgruntled minority factions bolted for new locations where they hoped to enforce their own rules and obtain better lands.

By 1640 the expanding settlements spawned new colonies. To the northeast, some Puritans settled along the coasts of New Hampshire and Maine, where they mingled uneasily with fishing folk, nominal Anglicans who came from the English West

Country. Southeastern New England became a haven for especially radical Puritan Separatists who settled around Narragansett Bay in independent towns that eventually made up the colony of Rhode Island. At the other religious extreme, some particularly conservative and ambitious Puritans found Massachusetts too lax in religion and too stingy in land grants. They proceeded southwest to found the colonies of Connecticut and New Haven along the Connecticut River and Long Island Sound. With 20,000 of the region's 33,000 inhabitants in 1660, Massachusetts remained the most populous, influential, and powerful of the New England colonies.

Later in the century, Rhode Island, Connecticut, and New Hampshire secured their own charters of government from the crown. Maine, New Haven, and Plymouth were less fortunate. In 1652, Maine's poor and vulnerable settlements accepted rule and protection by Massachusetts. In 1665, Connecticut absorbed the New Haven colony. In 1691, the crown issued a new charter for Massachusetts, extending its jurisdiction over Plymouth. That left four colonies in New England: Massachusetts, Connecticut, Rhode Island, and New Hampshire. . . .

Puritan Farms and Communities

The New England colonies granted lands to men who banded together as a corporate group to found a town. This town system contrasted with the Chesapeake colonies, where the leaders allocated land directly to individuals and usually in large tracts to the wealthy and well-connected. The Chesapeake practice dispersed settlement, which rendered it more difficult to sustain schools and churches and to repel Indian attacks. New English leaders favored relatively compact settlement in towns to concentrate people sufficiently for defense, to support public schools, to promote mutual supervision of morality, and, above all, to sustain a convenient and well-attended local church.

The colonial legislature defined the town boundaries but left to each town corporation the allocation of land for household farms and the location of a village center with church and school. More than simply a tract of land, the town was also a local government, fundamental to New England politics—in contrast to the Chesapeake colonies, which relied on the larger county.

Gathered in town meeting, the male property holders elected their local officials, principally a board of selectmen.

Favoring a gradual and modest distribution of land, the town founders initially awarded each household only ten to fifty acres (depending upon social status). Eventually, however, most seventeenth-century families acquired between one hundred and two hundred acres of farmland. Although about half the size of most Chesapeake plantations, the average New England farm was significantly larger than most landholdings in England, where few farmers owned so many as fifty acres and where over half the men possessed no land. And in New England almost all farmers enjoyed complete ownership, known as a freehold, in contrast to the leaseholds that prevailed in England. Freehold lands offered security from the rising rents charged by English landlords or Chesapeake great planters. The New English also avoided paying the quitrents charged by the lords proprietor or the crown in more southern colonies. A Puritan emigrant to New Jersey "swore—godzooks, he would have nothing to do with land as payed quitrents, for they paid none in New England."

To make farms, the colonists had to cut clearings in the forest, chop firewood, erect fences, build barns and houses, plow and plant fields, harvest crops, and construct mills—all from scratch by hand labor. This work was more demanding in cold and rocky New England than in the flatter, warmer, and fertile Chesapeake. And while demanding more labor to build, the New England farm generated smaller profits than the Chesapeake plantation. The shorter growing season and rougher land precluded the cultivation of the colonial staples in greatest European demand, tobacco and sugar. Instead, the New English farmers raised a northern medley of small crops—wheat, rye, maize, potatoes, beans, and garden plants. None could be profitably shipped for sale in England, where a similar climate permitted the same crops.

The New England farm family also tended a modest but critical herd of livestock—commonly two oxen, five other cattle, a horse, two sheep, and six pigs. Because livestock needed more land than grains, the New England farm had large pastures and hayfields but relatively small fields of grain. The farm families consumed most of their own crops and butchered animals or traded them for the goods and services of local artisans, principally carpenters, blacksmiths, and shoemakers. New England's diversified farms were less prone to disruption by the boom-and-bust price cycle than were the southern plantations specializing in a staple crop for an external market.

Unable to afford servants or slaves, the New English instead relied upon the family labor of their sons and daughters. A seventeenth-century Englishman reported, "Virginia thrives by keeping many servants, and these in strict obedience. New England [conceives that] they and their Children can doe enough, and soe [they] have rarely above one Servant." The healthy climate and good diet enabled parents to raise six or seven children to maturity. By age ten, boys worked with their fathers in the fields and barn, while daughters assisted their mothers in the house and garden. Most sons remained unmarried and working on the paternal farm until their middle or late twenties, retained by the prospect that their father could eventually provide each with a farm from the family rights in the town lands.

A Land of Rural Independence and Self-Sufficiency

Diligent and realistic, most New England families sought an "independent competency." "Independence" meant owning enough property—a farm or a shop—to employ a family, without having to work for someone else as a hired hand or servant. A "competency" meant a sufficiency, but not an abundance, of worldly goods: enough to eat, adequate if simple clothing, a roof over their heads, some consumer goods, and an ability to transmit this standard of living to many children. Although no land of riches, New England provided many independent farms and a secure household competency to hard and persistent labor. Edward Johnson of Massachusetts noted that even "the poorest person . . . hath a house and land of his own, and bread of his own growing, if not some cattel." Puritans regarded such a broad-based prosperity as more compatible with a godly life than the extremes of wealth and poverty found in England, the Chesapeake, and the West Indies. The Puritan minister John White observed, "Nothing sorts better with Piety than Competency."

Compared with those in the Chesapeake or West Indies, social gradations were subtle among the New English, who over-

whelmingly belonged to the middling sort. Their modest and diversified farms produced less wealth than did the staple plantations of the Chesapeake and the West Indies, but the New England economy distributed its rewards more equitably among
many farmers and tradesmen. In New English country towns the
leading men were substantial farmers, who worked with their
hands on properties only two or three times larger than the local average. And the leading rural men possessed few if any imported servants or slaves. The largest seaports—Boston, Salem,
and Newport—did host a wealthy elite of merchants, lawyers,
and land speculators. But they enjoyed less collective power than
did the great planters in the Chesapeake and West Indies, because the New England system of many nearly autonomous
towns dispersed political power in the countryside. Because New
England had the most decentralized and popularly responsive
form of government in the English empire, royalists despised the
region as a hotbed of "republicanism.". . .

The Bible Commonwealth: A Vision of a City on a Hill

More than the colonists in any other region, the orthodox New
English maintained that they had a divine mission to create a
model society in America: a Bible Commonwealth dedicated to
the proper worship of God and to the rules of a Godly society. As
Calvinists, the Puritans did not believe that publicly mandated
good behavior would lead people to heaven, but they hoped that
a moral society would abate God's wrath in this world, sparing
New England from famines, epidemics, wars, and other collective afflictions.

The Puritans believed that God held them to far higher standards than other, less godly people, that they reaped precious benefits and bore extraordinary burdens in New England because they
had entered into a close and particular contract, a "covenant,"
with God. As God's favored people, they considered themselves
the heirs to the ancient Israelites of the Old Testament. If they
honored his wishes, God would bestow health and abundance
upon them in this world. But should they deviate from his will in
any way, God would punish them as rebels—more severely than
he chastised common pagans, like the Indians.

Consequently, any hardship or setback called for a collective reassessment, and much individual soul-searching, to determine how they had disappointed God. And hardships and setbacks were frequent in the hard business of making new farms and new towns in a frontier setting an ocean removed from the hearth of their civilization. Profoundly insecure throughout the seventeenth century, the Puritans recurrently tried to recover the protective purity that they imagined had characterized their founding moment.

Moreover, as God's stronghold, Puritan New England invited relentless attack from Satan, who meant to destroy the Bible Commonwealth. Embroiled in the cosmic struggle between God's will and Satan's wiles, New England was a pivotal battleground for the eternal fate of all mankind. Puritans did not doubt the ultimate power and eventual triumph of God, but they also knew that, to castigate unwary humans, God permitted Satan to wax powerful on earth in the short term. No distant abstraction, the battle raged in every act and event that affected human life. Consequently, the Puritan authorities felt compelled to punish or exile people who seemed bent on the devil's work of destroying New England: sinners, dissidents, and witches. Otherwise, God would withdraw his favor and permit Satan the temporary triumph of destroying New England.

New England's Spiritual Life

Designed to please God, Puritan New England was a selective distillation from the more complex and conflicted culture of seventeenth-century England. The New English left behind many traditional customs and institutions that they believed offended God in England. By design, New England lacked church courts and tithes, bishops and archbishops, church weddings and ales, Sunday sports and maypoles, saint's days and Christmas. And except in rhetorical allegiance, there was no king. Rejecting much that was traditional to England, the Puritans promoted a Reformed culture that emphasized literacy and lay participation in governing congregations.

Puritans cherished direct access to holy and printed texts as fundamental to their liberty and identity as English and Protestant folk. They insisted that every individual should read the

Bible, rather than rely exclusively upon a priesthood for sacred knowledge. Almost every New England town sustained a public grammar school, and most women and almost all men could read—which was not the case in the mother country or in any other colonial region. And book ownership, primarily of Bibles and religious tracts, was more widespread in New England than anywhere else in the world. The New English imported most of their books from London, but they also established a press, the first in English America, at Cambridge, Massachusetts, in 1640. Possessed of print and the ability to read it, the common people of New England were far from passive recipients of religious instruction. Instead, they were demanding participants, active in the Christian discourse of their culture—often challenging and criticizing their ministers.

New England Puritans also had far more regular access to preaching than did any other English colonists. In 1650, Massachusetts had one minister for every 415 persons, compared with one per 3,239 persons in Virginia. By law every town had to sustain a church, supported by taxes levied on all the householders, whether members or not. And law required all inhabitants to attend midweek religious "lectures" and Sunday services, both morning and afternoon, each about two hours long. Puritan worship featured the minister's learned and forceful sermon based on a particular text of scripture. The average New English churchgoer heard about seven thousand sermons in the course of his or her lifetime. To train an orthodox Puritan ministry for so many churches, Massachusetts founded Harvard College in 1636—the first such institution in English America (the Spanish had already established several universities in their colonies). At mid-century Harvard graduates began to replace the founding generation of English-born ministers. . . .

Puritan Legacies in the Americas

New England ultimately failed as a "City upon a Hill," because the intended audience, the English, failed to pay attention. To most people at home, the Puritan experiment seemed at best strange and at worst seditious. New England appeared especially irrelevant after the triumphant restoration of the monarchy in 1660. The Restoration terminated and discredited the short-lived revolutionary regime led by English Puritans during the 1640s and 1650s. After the Restoration, English Puritans dwindled in number, prominence, and ambition. Most of the persistent made their peace with life as a quiet minority within an Anglican society. They dismissed New England as a distant and parochial backwater. In 1683 an English correspondent confessed to Cotton Mather, "I have often heard of New England, and long ago, but never took no great heed to it, only as persons do often discourse of things remote and at random."

New England Puritans blamed themselves for failing to inspire the mother country. During the later seventeenth century the New England clergy specialized in a genre of sermon known as the "jeremiad," named after the grim Old Testament prophet Jeremiah. A jeremiad catalogued the sufferings and sins of New England: the prevalence of Indian war, earthquakes, fires, and storms sent to punish a region wallowing in immorality and irreligion. Finding the present generation wanting, a jeremiad exhorted listeners to reclaim the lofty standards and pure morality ascribed to the founders of New England. Paradoxically, the popularity of the genre attested to the persistence, rather than the decline, of Puritan ideals in New England. Determined to live better, the laity longed for the cathartic castigation of the jeremiad. And the ministry complied with eloquence and zeal. But English Puritans often took the jeremiads at face value, confirming their unduly low estimation of New England.

In this literalism, those readers anticipated historians who reiterate the myth of a New England "declension" during the late seventeenth century. In fact, the overstated disappointment of the jeremiad was defined against an unrealistic and utopian depiction of the founders. The founding generation was, of course, far less perfect and united than it appeared in the mythic memory of the later generations. Naturally and necessarily, the orthodox New English culture and society *evolved* over the seventeenth century and into the eighteenth, but the core principles persisted, especially the commitment to a moral, educated, commercial, and homogeneous people. The formula of the jeremiad masked the prodigious long-term accomplishments of the New England colonists in substantiating their faith in dozens of churches, each with a college-educated minister committed to

Puritan ideals. The expensive construction and maintenance of so many churches and the long education of so many ministers—a commitment unmatched anywhere else in the English colonies—attested that the New English continued to yoke their economic achievements to their public faith. That the late-seventeenth-century New Englanders refused to take comfort or find reassurance in those accomplishments manifests how thoroughly Puritan they remained.

The myth of declension also obscures the prodigious and enduring Puritan legacy for English-speaking America. Compared with other colonial regions, New England was a land of relative equality, broad (albeit moderate) opportunity, and thrifty, industrious, and entrepreneurial habits that sustained an especially diverse and complex economy. The region's large, healthy families, nearly even gender ratio, and long life spans promoted social stability, the steady accumulation of family property, and its orderly transfer from one generation to the next. And nowhere else in colonial America did colonists enjoy readier access to public worship and nearly universal education. That those ideals remain powerful in our own culture attests to the enduring importance of the Puritan legacy.

Puritan Society: A Moral Role Model

Jonathan Edwards

Jonathan Edwards was a mid-eighteenth-century Puritan minister and intellectual who believed fervently in a highly orthodox, conservative interpretation of Puritan doctrine. In charge of ministerial duties in the commercial town of Northampton, Edwards, with his fiery preaching style and steadfast beliefs, revived spirituality in the community and gained it renown for its piety. In the following selection, an excerpt from a sermon to his congregation, Edwards reflects on the moral instruction that is provided by a strong, faithful Puritan society. Acknowledging his community as a "city on a hill," Edwards idealistically suggests that the Puritan people's lives are directed by God to serve as living examples of Christian virtue and good works.

We are as a city set upon an hill. . . . We are so by the distinguishing profession that we make. And we have been made so by the distinguishing and remarkable works that God hath wrought amongst us. And we have been made so by the great and remarkable influence that what has been seen and heard of amongst us, and the profession we make, has had on many other places. Though the whole work was the work of God, and we have nothing to attribute of it to ourselves; yet God was pleased evidently to make use of his own great and wonderful work here, as a means to stir up and awaken others all around us. And it has been improved by God as the occasion and means, whereby he has begun a great and wonderful work in many other places far and near. It has been with us very much as it was of old with the church of Thessalonica. I Thess. 1:7–8, "So that ye were ensamples to all that believe in Macedonia and Achaia. For from you sounded out the word of the Lord not only in Macedonia and Achaia, but also in every place your faith to God-ward is spread abroad."

The country in general was probably never so filled with talk

Jonathan Edwards, *Sermons and Discourses, 1734–1738,* edited by M.X. Lesser. New Haven, CT: Yale University Press, 2001.

of any work of such a nature. The fame of it spread abroad everywhere, and all sorts were earnestly inquiring about it. Some have inquired from real, hearty concern for the kingdom of God, and have heartily rejoiced to hear of such a work; and others have inquired from curiosity, because it was so strange and unusual a thing. Others have inquired from something of concern in their own minds: they have been a little startled, and their hearts something touched, by hearing the news of such a wonderful work of God. And others have inquired out of enmity against such a work. But the whole country has been filled, from one end of it to the other, with the fame of what has been here done, and what is here professed. And the eyes of all the land have been drawn upon us to observe us. And everyone has been inquiring, how the affair went on here; and after what manner the work was carried on; and what effect it has upon those that are the subjects of it, and how they behave themselves; and the like. So that there probably never was any town in this land, under so great obligations of that kind mentioned in the text and doctrine, to honor their profession by their practice as this town.

Here I would mention several things in particular respecting our being set as a city on an hill, which show our extraordinary obligation to adorn our profession by our practice.

The Devil Uses Many Devices to Thwart the Puritans

We may consider the great and violent endeavors that Satan has used to hinder the credit of the work that has been wrought amongst us. The devil has seemed extraordinarily to bestir himself to this purpose; for he knew that the bringing a reproach on this work of God would be the likeliest way to hinder the progress of it. Hell seems to be alarmed by the extraordinary breaking forth of the work of God here, and the sudden and swift propagation of it from town to town. The devils seem to have been all up in arms, if possible, to put a stop to it. And the way they have seemed chiefly to betake themselves to, has been to destroy the credit of the work; to hinder people abroad from believing that it was a good work; and to possess them with ill thoughts of it.

Thus you may remember that when the work was first begun in this town, that the neighboring towns seemed to be filled almost with talk against it. Many would speak contemptibly of it; some made a mean scoff and ridicule of it; and others that did not do so, yet seemed to suspect it. And when God notwithstanding carried on his work, and in a little time carried it into the neighboring towns, in spite of Satan's endeavors to prejudice them against it; then the devil seemed to be yet more alarmed, and to be more violent, and labored to bring a reproach on this work of God, by the violent onsets that he made on some particular persons, by extraordinary temptation to mischief and destroy themselves. In which God in his sovereign providence, was pleased to suffer him to prevail. . . .

And another device of Satan to hurt the credit of this work, by which he has been no less successful, has been to lead away and deceive some particular professors by enthusiastical impressions and imaginations; which they have conceited were divine revelations, such as were wont to be given to the prophets of old. And the noise of this has been swiftly spread abroad in the country, to the great wounding of the credit of the work of God in this part of the land. And another device of Satan to hinder the credit of this work, has been to fill the country with innumerable false and groundless reports. It has been astonishing to see how many strange and ridiculous stories have been carried abroad that have no foundation; and how that those things that have been in part true, that have been a blemish to religion amongst us, have been magnified and added to.

And another thing, wherein the spite and violence of Satan against the work of God here has been manifest, is the extraordinary means that have lately been used to cast an odium upon this county; and raise a kind of a mobbish rage and fury against the ministry of the county; and to prejudice the minds of the country against them, especially those of them that have chiefly stood in the defense of those truths of the gospel, in which the late work of God amongst us has mainly depended.

In this also God in his holy providence has suffered Satan to be in a great measure successful, as we have been well informed, to lessen the credit of the work of God amongst us.

And in all it has been very evident that Satan's spite has been chiefly against Northampton, if possible, to beget a prejudice in the minds of the country against this town, which has been the original and principal seat of this work of God. If Satan therefore be so great in his endeavors to bring a discredit on this work of God, certainly we that have been so peculiarly favored of God, ought to [be] great in our endeavors to uphold and promote the credit of it.

We may conclude that Satan knows that if this work be in credit, it will greatly tend to promote the glory of God, and the interest of religion; otherwise he would never so exert himself to hinder its being in credit. This should make us the more careful that we do nothing to discredit it, and that we do our utmost to promote the reputation of it.

And there is no way in the world that we can do so much, as by adorning our profession by our practice, and holding forth [to] the world the good and lovely fruits of this work of God. . . .

Faith and Good Works Reflect Well on Community Character

Consider how much it will be not only to the discredit of this particular work of God, but of all that kind of religion that we profess, if we don't walk according to our profession. It won't only make other people that behold us, and hear of us, question the truth of this work; but it will prejudice all talk or pretenses of such a work of conversion, as we profess the necessity of it, and against all such special experiences of the operations of the Spirit.

The land and the world are grown of late very much into prejudice against such sorts of things. It is quite contrary to that divinity that is lately everywhere fashionable.

And now in this work, there has been a notable instance given to the world of that which they are thus prejudiced against; and their eyes are very much drawn to see what this will come to. And if they see that there [are no] answerable fruits, it will exceedingly confirm 'em in their rejecting all such things, as being nothing but mere whimsy and enthusiasm. They have cried it down before, but then they will cry it down a great deal more. They will think they have demonstration against it. They will say, "There is the people at Northampton that experienced so much of such sorts of things. See what it comes to." And so all vital religion will suffer and come into discredit by our miscarriages. It seems so to be ordered in providence at present, that not only our own credit, and the credit of the late work of God amongst us, but the credit of all vital religion, and the power of godliness in this land, depends very much on the behavior of the people in this town; for the interest of religion depends on outward means.

Let me hence take occasion earnestly [to] address myself to all sorts amongst us, to consider these things, and to lay that weight on them that is due to them; and O, that it may [be] the earnest care of everyone to his utmost to watch over himself. Let us consider that the world has heard so much of a wonderful work of God amongst us, that they don't merely expect to hear of things that are negative amongst [us], and that we are a preferred people; but they will expect to hear something positive. What a good spirit there appears amongst us; how ready we are to [do] good works; how ready to deny ourselves; how forward to promote any good design; how charitable, and how public-spirited we be; how ready to lay out our substance for the poor, or for the worship of God, and the like.

I would entreat that there may be such a spirit as this manifest in the management of our public affairs, and not a backward, loth, fearful spirit, in that that is good; an over-fearfulness, lest we should spend too much; a disposition and aptness to quarrel for our money, lest too much of it should be laid out for public designs, and especially for the honor of God's public worship; and an aptness to have our spirits something on an edge, in opposition to them that differ from us in opinion, or are endeavoring to carry a contrary design. These things don't become a people that are as a city set on an hill, in the manner that we are.

Maintaining and Promoting Puritan Beliefs into the Future

And let me entreat that God may be honored and Christianity adorned in families. Let family orders and family religion be strictly kept up and attended. And don't let us have any custom of breaking of it, by being unseasonably absent from our home a-nights, or anything of that nature. And don't let us return to those disorders that we have forsaken—to frequenting the tavern; to night-walking, and frolicking, and rioting, and licentious company-keeping; to contending and quarreling. Don't let us, as the dog, return to this vomit or, as the sow that was washed, to wallowing in this filthy mire.

And here I would particularly direct myself to our young people. You are a generation that I hope are blessed of the Lord. I cannot but hope that many of you are beloved of God, are the objects of the dear love of God and the dying love of the Lord Jesus. That great blessing that God has lately poured out on this town, though it has descended on all sorts, yet has fallen more remarkably on your generation. Let me beseech you to hold fast that which you have received. Whereunto you have attained in escaping the pollutions of the world, therein abide. Don't return to any disorders, and licentious practices, or anything that is not of good report. Show yourselves ready to hearken to come and set as you have done, that you may be a generation to God's praise. Don't esteem the service of God your burden. Serve the Lord, and you will find that you serve a good master. Walk in wisdom's ways, and you will find you lose no pleasure by it.

When you are together, let your company be beautified and sweetened with religion and virtue, and in no wise tainted or sullied with anything vicious or extravagant.

I hope that many of you are the children of God. O, let me pray you to walk as becomes such. Walk not as the children of darkness, but as the children of the light and of the day. I Thess. 5:5, "Ye are all the children of light, and the children of the day: we are not of the night, nor of darkness"; Eph. 5:8, "For ye were sometimes darkness, but now are ye light in the Lord: walk as children of light." Love the Lord with all your hearts. Let him be the object of your highest love, and whatever love or friendship there be amongst you in anyone towards another. Let all be sanctified with the love of God.

And whatever company you keep one with another, let it not be marred and defiled by any manner of thing in word or deed that is lewd, or unchaste, or unseemly.

Let virtue and Christianity rule in your company-keeping, and let your society be improved for religious discourse. This will make your company and conversation together sweet to you in the time of it; and not only so, but sweet in your reflections on it, and sweet in the fruits of [it]. And you will find that nothing makes earthly love and company so sweet as the love of God, and the exercise of virtue and piety.

Educating the Youth Throughout the New World

Oscar Theodore Barck Jr. and Hugh Talmage Lefler

Oscar Theodore Barck Jr. earned acclaim as a professor and scholar in history at Syracuse University, and his colleague Hugh Talmage Lefler served as Kenan professor of history at the University of North Carolina. As the following selection suggests, the two historians are primarily interested in the cultural and economic aspects of early American life, rather than the more political aspects of settlement and conquest. The authors discuss the European roots of American educational practices and detail the differing methods of schooling in the middle, southern, and New England colonies. They cover a wide range of topics related to education and the transmittance of information and ideas, detailing the growth of higher education, the printing press, literature, and libraries in the colonies.

Education in America has always been the concern of the family, the church, and the government. In some of the colonies, particularly in the South where there were few towns and population was widely dispersed, education was left largely to parents. They taught their own children or, in the case of the more affluent families, employed tutors or paid the tuition of their children in some "subscription" school or other private educational agency. In other sections, notably the Middle colonies, various churches maintained "parochial schools" to minister to their adherents. In New England a policy of direct public responsibility developed, though the church and the family continued to exert great influence on educational policies and practices. The diversity of educational systems in the various regions and individual colonies, as well as the rate of progress in establishing and maintaining schools and colleges, bore a close relationship to such factors as religion, density of population, wealth, and the educational background and interest of church leaders and government officials.

Diverse Teaching Styles Have Roots in England

In all the colonies, regardless of the agency responsible for schools, education, in conjunction with many social and political ideals, reflected the influence of the English background. Education in the mother country was for the privileged few, not for the masses. The state made no direct contribution to the many private and endowed elementary schools, though the teachers were licensed by the king or a bishop of the Established Church. The apprenticeship system prevailed for poor children, who never received any "book learning," but who nevertheless were given practical instruction in a large variety of trades. In 1600 there were about 360 privately or Church-endowed "Latin Grammar" or secondary schools, such as Eton and Harrow, which had religious requirements for admission and whose curricula emphasized classical and religious subjects. The various colleges at Oxford and Cambridge dominated higher education, but these institutions were under Church control; they admitted only communicants of the Anglican Church and had clerical faculties. Their purposes were primarily "the training of scholars, statesmen, and church leaders."

Education in New England

It is not surprising that the Massachusetts Bay Colony was the pioneer in colonial education. The Puritans who came to the colony, especially those who arrived in the twenty years after 1630, were convinced that they had a "divine mission" and that an obligation rested upon them to be "fit vessels of the Lord." The opening sentence of Edward Johnson's *New England's First Fruits* (1643) declared:

> After God had carried us safe to *New England*, and wee had builded our houses, provided necessaries four our liveli-hood, rear'd convenient places for Gods worship, and setled the Civill Government: One of the next things we longed for, and looked

after was to advance *Learning* and perpetuate it to Posterity; dreading to leave an illiterate Ministry in the Churches, when our present Ministers shall lie in the Dust.

But there were other reasons for the priority of Massachusetts in education. The leaders, themselves educated (about one of each two hundred of the first generation was college-trained), desired similar opportunities for others; the people lived in fairly compact communities, largely in towns and villages; ministers had to be trained to give the settlers proper religious instruction to perpetuate the Bible Commonwealth; and, what was very important, adequate governmental and personal income facilitated educational opportunities.

The citizens of Boston took the initial step when they held a mass meeting in the spring of 1635, elected "our brother Mr. Philemon Pormort" as schoolmaster, and established a school later called the Boston Public Latin School. Next, Massachusetts law of 1642 required parents to have their children taught to "read & understand the principles of religion & capitall lawes of this country," to write, and to learn a trade. General supervision of such training was entrusted to town officials. Because many parents had too many other cares or too little education and wealth themselves to discharge their duties properly, a law was enacted in 1647 establishing a free school system and compulsory attendance. Every town with fifty families was required to establish an elementary school, and each town with one hundred families must establish a grammar school "to instruct youth so far as they shall be fitted for the university." The purpose of this measure, as stated in the preamble, was to prevent the "ould deluder Satan" from keeping "men from the Knowledge of the Scriptures." The principle of state responsibility embodied in these laws was gradually extended throughout New England.

Many towns established Latin Grammar Schools and a few had special "writing schools." These institutions were financed by tuition and other fees, donations, and funds voted by town or colonial government. Each school had one teacher or "master," though the Boston Latin School and perhaps a few others had an additional instructor, called the "usher." As the name implied, emphasis was placed on Latin, with the idea of preparation for college. As only a small number of graduates went on to college, the Latin School gradually lost favor. The laws relating to these schools were also laxly enforced, as evidenced by the report of the Massachusetts legislature in 1701 that the school statutes were "shamefully neglected in divers towns." In some communities, the academy—a private school for the wealthier classes offering broader instruction and more practical subjects—began to replace the old Latin Grammar School, particularly after the middle of the eighteenth century.

When a community was not able or willing to provide regular schools, an effort to educate the young was frequently made in "dame schools," conducted in the home of some housewife who taught children to read and write. This type was, in a sense, a day-nursery and elementary school combined. It afforded some women an opportunity to earn a little money, and it was the means by which many youngsters learned some of the rudiments of education.

In schools of almost every type children learning to read followed "the ordinary road of Hornbook, Primer, Psalter, Testament, and Bible." Pupils learned to read by using a "hornbook," which was not a book at all, but a flat piece of wood—or sometimes of leather—with a handle, on the face of which was a piece of paper or parchment covered by a thin, transparent sheet of horn. This device usually contained the letters of the alphabet, numerals, and sometimes a list of vowels and syllables, and perhaps the Lord's Prayer. *The New England Primer*, prepared by Benjamin Harris, a London printer, and published in Boston about 1690, was the first textbook printed in the colonies. This book was "for one hundred years *the* schoolbook of the dissenters of America, and for another hundred years was frequently reprinted." One of its features was the rhymed alphabet; an example was:

A—In *Adam's* Fall
    We Sinned all.

G—As runs the *Glass*
    Man's life doth pass.

T—*Time* cuts down all
    Both great and small.

In schools at all levels, emphasis was placed on "memory

work" or "learning by heart." There was little opportunity for freedom of thought or expression—no "projects" or "activity" or "progressive education." The colonists everywhere took seriously the axioms: "Spare the rod and spoil the child" and "Love well, whip well." Accordingly, discipline in the home and at school, usually in the form of flogging, was administered in large doses. Perhaps obedience to teachers and respect for parental authority were carried too far, but the fact remains that the colonists never had any serious problem of juvenile delinquency.

Schools in the Middle Colonies

Educational progress in the Middle colonies was slower than in New England, and more varied types of schools developed, the result of such factors as national diversity, language differences, economic interests, and the attitude of Quakers and some other sects toward education. . . .

Quaker influence dominated education in colonial Pennsylvania. Despite the statement by George Fox, founder of his sect, that "God stands in no need of human learning," an early law required parents to have children taught reading and writing. The statute was not enforced, and no "public schools" were established. There were, however, a number of Quaker-sponsored schools, among them the William Penn Charter School, begun in 1689 and chartered in 1697. These schools placed less emphasis on the classics and more on English, mathematics, and such "practical studies" as bookkeeping and surveying than did most of the schools of early America.

Education in the South

The diffusion of population, the planters' views on education, and the attitude of the Established Church were all deterrents to the development of public schools in the Southern colonies. Some of the aristocrats, though not all, perhaps agreed with the famous statement of Governor William Berkeley: "Thank God there are no schools and no printing presses in Virginia and I hope there will be none for these hundred years." The Anglican Church was hostile to schools under control of "dissenters," and until the middle of the eighteenth century the Southern colonies relied largely on tutors and private schools sponsored by the Anglican clergy. In the last two decades of the colonial period a number of Presbyterian-backed academies and seminaries were founded, but these institutions failed to reach the masses; they provided instead classical and professional training for the higher classes. The chief types of private schools were the "old field" schools—so called because they were located on abandoned farm land—which stressed elementary subjects, and the academies, which taught not only some elementary courses, but also college preparatory studies in the classics, science, mathematics, and literature.

Children of the wealthier people were usually given instruction in the home and then sent to some colonial college or to England. The children of the poor, and especially orphans and illegitimate children, received a limited education through the agencies of indentured servitude and the apprenticeship system. Masters and guardians were required by law to give their wards the "rudiments of learning" and teach them a "useful trade." Orphans were also to be taught "according to rank and degree."

Such formal schooling as existed in any colony was largely confined to boys. Girls might sometimes attend primary schools, though mostly in off seasons, or learn to read and write in dame schools. Usually, however, they were taught at home to do "those things which would make them a good wife and housekeeper."

Colonial Colleges

The most remarkable feature of colonial education was the establishment of colleges even before any foundation for primary and secondary education had been laid. This unusual situation may be attributed largely to four causes: the importance of college-trained men among the first settlers, especially in New England; the interest in and need for trained clergymen; the education of a large number of colonial lawyers at the Inns of Court in London; and the interest of many churches, merchants, and planters in the education of the "better sort."

Virginia was the first to propose erection of a college, but it was Massachusetts that actually established the first college in what is now the United States. In 1636 the legislature of Massachusetts agreed to give £400 towards a "Schoole or Colledge, whereof

£200 to be paid the next year and £200 when the work is finished." A year later the legislature ordered the college erected at Newtown, and the year after that changed the name of Newtown to Cambridge, in honor of the college town in England. About the same time the name of the institution was changed to Harvard, because John Harvard, a Charlestown minister, bequeathed his library and part of his estate to the institution.

Harvard's first head (who was called "professor," not "president"), Nathaniel Eaton, though "recommended for his knowledge of theology," almost starved the students, misused college funds, whipped some of his assistants, and finally fled to Virginia, where, according to John Winthrop, he succumbed to vice, "being usually drunken, as the custom is there."

Despite this unfortunate incident, the college recovered and soon became a "nursery of learning and a training school" for Puritan preachers. The curriculum, based largely on that of Emmanuel College, Cambridge, England, consisted chiefly of Latin, Greek, Hebrew, logic, ethics, and rhetoric—proper subjects for ministerial candidates. There was little attention to mathematics and the natural sciences, and none to history and modern languages. This course of study set the general pattern for most of the colonial colleges until about 1765, though the curriculum of William and Mary followed that of the University of Edinburgh, alma mater of its founder and first president, James Blair, and Philadelphia Academy and College (later the University of Pennsylvania), the one colonial college not founded specifically under church auspices, made a radical departure in its curriculum when it offered science, mathematics, modern languages, and history as early as 1754. . . .

Student Life

Academic mortality among college students was low. Fewer than six hundred entered Harvard prior to 1700, but 465 were graduated. It appeared that "if a student attended classes regularly, paid his fees, and observed the proper deportment," he would receive his diploma. The number of college graduates increased rapidly in the eighteenth century. In the thirty-year period 1715–1745 there were fourteen hundred persons who successfully completed their college training, and between 1745 and 1775 there were more than three thousand.

The college day was long, from dawn to dusk. Classes were held throughout the day. Students were expected to recite frequently and to elaborate on their texts. Lectures by the faculty were usually delivered only to seniors. Prayers were compulsory both morning and evening, and on Sundays the church of the student's choice must be attended. "Cutting classes" was frowned upon and might result in fines. Library facilities were meager, and the students did not take full advantage of those that were available. At the end of the colonial period Harvard had about four thousand volumes, Yale almost as many, and the remaining college libraries contained fewer than three thousand.

The students were expected to reside in the college hall—there were not more than two or three buildings on the entire college "campus"—with two or three in a room, and to eat in the college refectory. The normal breakfast consisted principally of bread and butter, the main meal of meat and potatoes was served in the middle of the day, and at night "leftovers" were the fare.

There were no fraternities—though there might be "literary societies"—no organized athletics, and no regular extracurricular activities to divert the students from the major task of obtaining an education. But boys away from home then, as now, occasionally played pranks, for which they were frequently fined and even flogged. One method of giving vent to surplus energies was to haze freshmen; at Harvard they had to run any errands demanded by upperclassmen. Once in a while pranks got out of hand, provoking public criticism. For example, the Reverend Solomon Stoddard found fault with the situation at Harvard during the course of a sermon in 1703:

> Places of learning should not be places of riot. . . . Ways of profusion and prodigality in such a society lay a foundation of a great deal of sorrow. . . . 'Tis not worth the while for persons to be sent to the College to learn to compliment men and court women; they should be sent thither to prepare them for public service and had need to be under the oversight of holy men.

The student uprising at Harvard in 1766, known as the "butter rebellion," received much adverse publicity, and the student body at Yale in one instance demonstrated so vociferously that President Thomas Clap was compelled to resign.

Toward the close of the colonial period more and more young men from the Southern colonies attended colleges in the North, notably King's College and the College of New Jersey. The result was the partial breakdown of provincialism and the development of a greater spirit of colonial unity. A large number of the leaders in church and state, perhaps the majority in the late colonial and Revolutionary era, were college-trained. Of the fifty-four signers of the Declaration of Independence, eighteen had attended some institution of higher learning. Seldom in American history have so few educated men wielded so much influence. Especially noteworthy was the role of college men in the political developments that were climaxed by the American Revolution, separation from the British Empire, and the establishment of the United States under the Constitution.

At the same time, however, there were widespread ignorance and illiteracy among the masses. In 1775 John Adams declared that a native inhabitant who could read was "as rare as a comet or an earthquake." The major effort to remedy this educational deficiency occurred at the time of the Revolution, when several states wrote into their constitutions the principles of public education. It was not until well into the next century, however, that most of the states actually translated these constitutional mandates into action by the creation of "common schools" supported by public taxation.

The Press Has a Large Impact on Learning and the Transmission of Information

Despite the paucity of formal educational opportunities, American colonists, especially in the urban communities, possessed numerous outlets for intellectual activity. After 1700 one of the most important of these was the newspaper. The printing press made its appearance in some colonies at a relatively early date— in Massachusetts in 1639—but the primary reason for its establishment was the necessity of printing and circulating the laws. Almost a century elapsed before there was a regular newspaper. In the autumn of 1689 Samuel Green of Boston published a "news-letter" called *The Present State of New English Affairs*, which some have called the first American newspaper; others reserve that honor for Benjamin Harris, also of Boston, who printed in

1690 a four-page paper, or pamphlet, entitled *Public Occurrences, both Foreign and Domestick,* which was suppressed after one issue because of "reflections of a very high nature" on a current political issue. . . .

The typical colonial newspaper was a weekly, and the subscription price varied. . . . It usually consisted of four pages and was about the size of a modern tabloid. It contained a small amount of gossip and local news, and such items as shipping notices, customhouse clearings and entries, domestic and foreign letters, speeches of governors, important acts of Parliament, and reprints from other journals, especially English publications. There was more advertising—of land, books, runaway slaves, imported articles—than is commonly supposed, and it was scattered all over the paper, including the first page. There were few or no editorials in most of the papers, though a considerable amount of editorial opinion was expressed indirectly. There were no comic strips, sports pages, or society columns. Most papers had no cartoons, although one of the first significant ones was Franklin's snake cut into eight pieces, with the caption "Join or Die," which appeared at the time of the French and Indian War. Newspapers had no "front page" in the modern journalistic sense of that term, nor large headlines, though there were some variations in the size of type. The type in many newspapers was bad, but the paper, made from linen rags, was excellent. One person, often the editor himself, sometimes with the aid of a "printer's devil," did all the work of getting out the journal: collecting "news," selling advertising, setting type, and eliciting subscriptions. Sometimes the editor was also the public printer, the postmaster, the operator of a bookstore, and the like. . . .

Colonial Literature

The old views that the colonial era produced little literature worthy of the name prior to the pre-Revolutionary decade, and that Jonathan Edwards and Benjamin Franklin were about the only writers of note, have undergone considerable modification in recent years. To be sure, there was little "creative writing," few or no professional writers, and no great novels, short stories, dramas, poems, or studies of "social problems." Yet, there were hundreds of vigorous, plain, matter-of-fact, and highly readable narratives: travel accounts, diaries and journals, and histories, written by the actual participants in "the making of America." And what colonial literature lacked in quality was more than made up in quantity. The output of some of the writers, who were also busily engaged in other pursuits, was phenomenal. A large number of promoters of colonization, such as [William] Bradford, [John] Winthrop, John Smith, [Roger] Williams, and [William] Penn, had from one to a dozen books each to their credit. The father-and-son combination of Increase and Cotton Mather published some six hundred titles.

In the seventeenth century the major theme of writers, especially in New England, was religion, or rather, theological and ecclesiastical subjects. In other areas, and to some extent even in New England, there were many men who wrote travel accounts and diary-histories about fearful sea voyages, adventures in the wilderness, famine, disease, warfare, "Indian captivities," "wonderful deliverances," "God's Protecting Providence," and even about the "lot of servants in the New World." The eighteenth century witnessed a considerable increase in the variety and quality of publications. More history was written—some of it of good quality—more attention was given to political matters as the Revolution approached, and there appeared works on scientific subjects. . . .

Literature in early America "clung to hard fact." People wrote about what they saw, heard, and thought, the best foundations for good writing at any time. Modern scholars may say that the numerous historical accounts of this period were not "scientific," but the fact remains that these very critics have drawn heavily upon those writings. And no so-called scientific historian has ever given a more beautiful definition of history than the one by Captain John Smith, that "History is the memory of time, the life of the dead, the happiness of the living."

Books and Libraries

From the beginning of settlement, books played an important part in the cultural development of the colonies, especially in New England. Many of the first immigrants brought along their little libraries, and the more affluent ones continued to import books from London. Booksellers, who were frequently publishers as well, could provide European publications of every description.

Some men accumulated substantial libraries, the largest being that of William Byrd II of Westover, Virginia, amounting to four thousand volumes. The libraries usually contained books in the fields of theology, philosophy, political economy, history, general literature, law, and medicine. Greek and Roman writers were frequently represented; some of the works of Shakespeare, Milton, Bacon, Locke, Voltaire, Swift, Addison, Steele, and other prominent contemporary authors were likewise to be found. A few of the larger libraries often contained copies of leading English periodicals, notably *The Spectator, The Tatler* and *The Annual Register.*

In addition to the private collections of books, there were some semiprivate "public libraries." Mention has already been made of the parochial libraries sent to a number of the colonies. . . . The increasing interest in books and the general cultural progress of the eighteenth century, however, were reflected in the formation of public libraries, the first at Charleston, South Carolina, shortly after the legislature authorized such an institution in 1700, and the more famous subscription library sponsored by Benjamin Franklin at Philadelphia in 1731. By the time of the Revolution there were many libraries—public, subscription, parish, and college. The increased interest in reading and writing in the late colonial period is closely related to the fact that the American Revolution has been called "the most literate war" ever fought.

The First American University

Cotton Mather

Cotton Mather (1663–1728) wanted his writings to revive Puritan zeal and celebrate God. A grandson of the founders of the first established colony in New England and son to famous Boston preacher Increase Mather, Cotton was destined to play a role in the puritanical development of New England. He served as minister at Boston's historical Old North Church for over forty years and attended America's first university, Harvard College, an institution that he honors in the following selection. In this writing, Mather details how the college was established and funded and depicts various aspects of collegiate life. Mather upholds the university as a place to nurture both the spiritual and academic potential in young men and uses it as an example to illustrate the cultural growth of the American people.

The nations of mankind, that have shaken off barbarity, have not more differed in the languages, than they have agreed in this one principle, that *schools*, for the institution of young men, in all other liberal sciences, as well as that of languages, are necessary to procure, and preserve, that learning amongst them, which [chastens the manners and the soul refines] . . .

A General Court, held at Boston, September 8, 1630, advanced a small sum (and it was then a day of small things), namely, four hundred pounds, by way of essay towards the building of something to begin a Colledge; and New-Town being the [City of Books] appointed for the seat of it, the name of the town was for the sake of somewhat now founding here, which might hereafter grow into an University, changed into Cambridge. 'Tis true, the University of Upsal in Sueden hath ordinarily about seven or eight hundred students belonging to it, which do none of them live collegiately, but board all of them here and there at private

Cotton Mather, *Magnalia Christi Americana; or, the Ecclesiastical History of New-England*. New York: Russell and Russell, 1967.

houses; nevertheless, the government of New-England was for having their students brought up in a more collegiate way of living. But that which laid the most significant *stone* in the foundation, was the last will of Mr. JOHN HARVARD, a reverend and excellent minister of the gospel, who, dying at Charlestown of a consumption, quickly after his arrival here, bequeathed the sum of seven hundred, seventy nine pounds, seventeen shillings and two pence, towards the pious work of building a Colledge, which was now set a foot. A committee then being chosen, to prosecute an affair so happily commenced, it soon found encouragement from several other benefactors: the other colonies sent some small help to the undertaking, and several particular gentlemen did more than whole colonies to support and forward it: but because the memorable Mr. JOHN HARVARD led the way by a generosity exceeding the most of them that followed, *his* name was justly æternized, by its having the name of HARVARD COLLEDGE imposed upon it.

The Colonial University Could Be Cruel

While these things were a doing, a society of scholars, to lodge in the *new nests*, were forming under the conduct of one Mr. Nathaniel Eaton, [or, if thou wilt, reader, *Orbilius* Eaton] a blade who marvellously deceived the expectations of good men concerning him; for he was one fitter to be master of a Bridewel than a Colledge; and though his *avarice* was notorious enough to get the name of a [money-lover] fixed upon him, yet his *cruelty* was more scandalous than his *avarice*. He was a rare scholar himself, and he made many more such; but their education truly was "in the school of Tyrannus." Among many other instances of his cruelty, he gave one in causing two men to hold a young gentleman, while he so unmercifully beat him with a *cudgel*, that, upon complaint of it unto the court in September, 1639, he was fined an hundred marks, besides a convenient sum to be paid unto the young gentleman that had suffered by his unmercifulness; and for his inhumane severities towards the scholars, he was removed from his trust. After this, being first excommunicated by the church of Cambridge, he did himself excommunicate all our churches going first into Virginia, then into England, where he lived privately until the restauration of King Charles the II. Then

conforming to the ceremonies of the church of England, he was
fixed at Biddiford, where he became a bitter persecutor of the
Christians that kept faithful to the way of worship, from which
he was himself an apostate; until he who had cast so many into
prison for *conscience*, was himself cast into prison for *debt;* where
he did, at length, pay one debt namely, that unto *nature*, by death.

Benefactors' Good Works and Public Donations Establish College

On August 27, 1640, the magistrates, with the ministers, of the
colony, chose Mr. Henry Dunstar to be the President of their new
Harvard-Colledge. And in time convenient, the General Court
endued the Colledge with a charter, which made it a corporation,
consisting of a President, two Fellows, and a Treasurer to all
proper intents and purposes: only with powers reserved unto the
Governour, Deputy-Governour, and all the magistrates of the
colony, and the ministers of the six next towns for the time being, to act as *overseers* or *visitors* of the society. The tongues and
arts were now taught in the Colledge, and piety was maintained
with so laudable a discipline, that many eminent persons went
forth from hence, adorned with accomplishments, that rendered
them formidable to other parts of the world, as well as to this
country, and persons of good quality sent their sons from other
parts of the world for such an education as this country could
give unto them. The number of benefactors to the Colledge did
herewithal increase to such a degree of benefits, that although
the President were supported still by a salary from the Treasury
of the colony, yet the Treasury of the Colledge itself was able to
pay many of its expences; especially after the incomes of
Charlestown ferry were by an act of the General Court settled
thereupon. To enumerate these benefactors would be a piece of
justice to their memory, and the catalogue of their names and
works, preserved in the Colledge, has done them that justice. But
as I find one article in that catalogue to run thus, "a gentleman
not willing his name should be put upon record, gave fifty
pounds;" thus I am so willing to believe, that most of those good
men that are mentioned were content with a record of their good
deeds in the book of God's remembrance, that I shall excuse this
book of our church history from swelling with a particular men-

tion of them: albeit for us to leave unmentioned in this place MOULSON, a SALTONSTAL, an ASHURST, a PENNOYER, a DODDRIDGE, an HOPKINS, a WEB, an USHER, an HULL, a RICHARDS, an HULTON, a GUNSTON, would hardly be excusable. And while these made their liberal contributions, either to the edifice or to the revenue of the Colledge, there were others that enriched its library by present-ing of choice books with mathematical instruments thereunto, among whom Sir Kenelm Digby, Sir John Maynard, Mr. Richard Baxter, and Mr. Joseph Hill, ought always to be remembered. But the most considerable accession to this library was, when the Reverend Mr. Theophilus Gale, a well known *writer* of many books, and *owner* of more, bequeathed what he had unto his New-English treasury of learning; whereof I find in an Oration of Mr. Increase Mather, at the commencement in the year 1681, this commemoration:—[The library of Harvard College is en-riched with a great number of books, and those such as are best worth reading—selected by Theophilus Yale, (of blessed mem-ory) who has never yet received his full meed of praise as a the-ologian; also, by William Stoughton, the Moses of the New Eng-landers, who was the first benefactor of this institution, and has bound all true sons of Harvard to himself in bonds of everlasting gratitude.] Indeed this library is at this day, far from a Vatican, or a Bodleian dimension, and sufficiently short of that made by Ptolemy at Alexandria, in which *Fame* hath placed seven hun-dred thousand volumes, and of that made by Theodosius at Con-stantinople, in which a more certain *fame* hath told us of ten myriads: nevertheless 'tis I suppose the best furnished that can be shown any where in all the American regions. . . .

Expectations and Requirements of Harvard Men

When scholars had so far profitted at the grammar schools that they could read any classical author into English, and readily make and speak true Latin, and write it in *verse* as well as *prose;* and perfectly decline the *paradigms* of nouns and verbs in the Greek tongue, they were judged capable of admission in Harvard-Colledge; and, upon the examination, were accordingly admit-ted by the President and Fellows; who, in testimony thereof, signed a copy of the Colledge laws, which the scholars were each

of them to transcribe and preserve, as the continual remem-
brancers of the duties whereto their priviledges obligded them.
While the *President* inspected the *manners* of the students thus entertained in the Colledge, and unto his morning and evening
prayers in the hall joined an *exposition* upon the chapters; which
they read out of Hebrew into Greek, from the *Old* Testament in
the morning, and out of English into Greek, from the *New* Testament in the evening; besides what Sermons he saw cause to
preach in publick assemblies on the Lord's day at Cambridge
where the students have a particular gallery allotted unto them;
the Fellows resident on the place became Tutors to the several
classes, and after they had instructed them in the Hebrew language, led them through all the *liberal arts*, ere their first *four years*
expired. And in this time, they had their weekly *declamations*, on
Fridays in the Colledge-hall, besides publick *disputations*, which
either the President or the Fellows moderated. Those who then
stood candidates to be graduates, were to attend in the hall for
certain hours, on Mondays, and on Tuesdays, three weeks together towards the middle of June, which were called "weeks of
visitation;" so that all comers that pleased might examine their
skill in the *languages* and *sciences* which they now pretended unto;
and usually, some or other of the overseers of the Colledge would
on purpose *visit* them, whilst they were thus doing what they
called "sitting of solstices:" when the *commencement* arrived—
which was formerly the second Tuesday in August, but since, the
first Wednesday in July—they that were to proceed Bachelors,
held their *act* publickly in Cambridge; whither the magistrates and
ministers, and other gentlemen then came, to put respect upon
their exercises: and these exercises were, besides an oration usually made by the President, orations both *salutatory* and *valedic-
tory*, made by some or other of the commencers, wherein all *persons* and *orders* of any fashion then present, were addressed with
proper complements, and reflections were made on the most remarkable occurrents of the præceding year; and these orations
were made not only in Latin, but sometimes in Greek and in Hebrew also; and some of them were in verse, and even in Greek
verse, as well as others in prose. But the main exercises were *disputations* upon questions, wherein the *respondents* first made their
theses: for according to Vossius, the very essence of the Baccalau-

reat seems to lye in the thing: BACCALAUREUS being but a name corrupted of *Batualius*, which *Batualius* (as well as the French *Bataile*) comes *a Batuendo*, a business that carries *beating* in it: So that, [They were called *Battailers*, because they had battled as it were with an antagonist—that is, had engaged in a public controversy or discussion, and thus given a specimen of their proficiency.] In the close of the day, the President, with the formality of delivering a book into their hands, gave them their *first degree*.

Colonial Entertainment

CHAPTER

3

Chapter Preface

Colonial Americans made most of their own fun. Although life was difficult and it was a struggle to survive, the colonists did in fact take time to socialize and play games. Whereas the cultures of the southern and middle colonies were more apt to social celebration, even the Puritans, whose moralistic ideals forbade gambling, the consumption of alcohol, and dancing, did not restrict all forms of entertainment.

Young boys and girls played rhyming and counting games. Games still popular today, such as tag and "I Spy," were also popular. Boys were especially interested in marbles, and they went sledding, ice-skating, flew kites, swam, and ran footraces. Girls often played with dolls carved out of cornhusks or small bits of wood. Quilting and embroidering taught girls important lessons as well as entertained them.

Beyond quilting and sewing, other necessary kinds of work were turned into games and sports. Boys often went hunting, fishing, and crabbing. They had fishing competitions, and youths old enough to fire guns entered shooting contests. Men also competed in such games of skill, having archery, hunting, and wrestling tournaments for both practice and amusement. Very popular and cruel sports often gained men's attention during this time. Cockfighting and bullbaiting (a process in which a bull or bear is tied to a stake and attacked by hunting dogs) are examples of these pastimes.

Despite the fact that women worked long, hard, difficult days in colonial America, they were considered too delicate and ladylike to participate in many of the sports or activities mentioned above. With the exception of ice-skating, these amusements were in the male realm. Because of this, women found their entertainment in the domestic sphere. Outside of restrictive Puritan New England, they organized dances, entertained huge formal dinners, played musical instruments, and enjoyed other similar pursuits.

Many games popularized in colonial times remain well liked today. The game of ninepins, introduced by the Dutch, closely resembles the modern game of bowling. And a game called

Quoits, in which a metal ring is tossed at a distant target, parallels the contemporary pastime of horseshoes. The Native Americans introduced the games of lacrosse and shinny, which is comparable to hockey, to the European consciousness.

Though basic and rudimentary, colonial games anticipate many contemporary American pastimes and reveal a good deal about their society. As many of the examples indicate, the colonists made an effort to turn their work into play and contests in order to bring a degree of levity to their strenuous lives. Their games demonstrate the colonists' ingenuity, desire for fun and diversions, and their competitive attitude.

The Colonial Stage

Hugh F. Rankin

Although it took some time for theaters to gain acceptance in the American colonies, largely because of strict religious views, the plays that were performed reflect colonial America's ties to European culture and the New World's prejudices and belief systems. In the following selection, Hugh F. Rankin, a professor of history at Tulane University and an author/editor of many books on colonial American life, discusses the varying reactions to the theater in the colonies. He details the earliest plays, actors, and playwrights that helped initiate this important feature of American culture.

L eisure time activities in England's American colonies, as in all colonial cultures, were quite naturally patterned after those of the mother country, although there was always the time lag occasioned by overseas expansion. Through the years, English dramatists had gradually modified the theater from an aristocratic to a middle-class institution, but the favor of the upper class was by no means alienated. As such, it was more readily acceptable to the American colonists, who were themselves modifying an English heritage into a culture that would one day be termed "American.". . .

Though They Struggled, Colonial Theaters Survived

Despite early vigorous opposition waged against the theater in the American colonies, resistance was gradually worn down except in New England, where Puritan convictions remained as steadfast as the boulders of her rock-bound coast. There, hostility to the drama was so firmly entrenched that only the erosion of the passing years and changing times could wear it down. Even in the other colonies, laws restricting theatrical activities were sometimes passed as a sop to religious extremists but just

Hugh F. Rankin, *The Theater in Colonial America.* Chapel Hill: University of North Carolina Press, 1965. Copyright © 1960 by the University of North Carolina Press. Reproduced by permission of the publisher.

as often were ignored. Only Virginia and Maryland never enacted legislation prohibiting the theater, and it was in Virginia
that the theater was able to gain its first foothold in America. . . .

The limitations of the colonial theater are obvious. It was derivative in nature; it produced practically no playwrights; and its
stylized acting ignored the more natural innovations introduced
to the English stage by [actor] David Garrick. But it did bring a
lively and vigorous entertainment from the Old World to the
New and demonstrated that a tiny colonial capital, such as
Williamsburg or Annapolis, could sustain one of the important
ornaments of civilized life, a repertory theater. To call the colonial theater derivative is not to damn it—indeed, all colonial cultures are, by their very natures, derivative. . . .

Popular Plays and Playwrights

Despite the performances of new plays written for the London
stage, William Shakespeare was the most popular playwright
with American playgoers. Again, this was a reflection of English
tastes, the overseas transplanting of the Georgian revival of
Shakespeare, of which someone has said:

> After one hundred and thirty years' nap,
> Enter Shakespeare with a loud clap.

In the twenty-four years before the Revolution, fourteen of his
plays were performed at least 180 times, and, in the light of the
paucity of information, it would be reasonable to guess the total
to be at least 500. Shakespeare was performed in the altered ver-
sions played on the London stage. Of the fourteen plays, only
two seem to have been presented in anything like their original
form, and even those two were cut to fit into an abbreviated
playing time. Although it was felt that Shakespeare's greatest
forte lay in his facility "to interest the minds of an audience,"
managers did not hesitate to insert "vile and degrading interpo-
lations," so that "little of the creative powers of Shakespeare is
to be seen in it."

On the American stage, *Richard III* and *Romeo and Juliet* were
the two Shakespeare favorites and were presented more than
any contemporary tragedy. David Garrick's alterations of the
Bard's works seem to have been most favored by the American

comedians, even though it has been said of them that they were "sometimes the reverse of creditable." His adaptation of *The Taming of the Shrew*, retitled *Catherine and Petruchio*, was often selected as an afterpiece to accompany *Romeo and Juliet*, which, of course, featured the popular and gaudy funeral procession to the tomb of the Capulets.

After Shakespeare's works, the most popular play in the colonies was George Lillo's *George Barnwell*, sometimes said to have been the first honest attempt to correct, from the stage, the vices and weaknesses of mankind. This piece, depicting the temptations of a young man to steal and murder because of his infatuation for an unscrupulous woman, brought domestic middleclass tragedy into fashion, and one lady was quoted in the *Gentleman's Magazine* as saying that "none but a prostitute could find fault with this tragedy." In the colonies, it was always a wise selection in those communities that exhibited hostility towards

Adaptations of Shakespeare's plays, such as The Taming of the Shrew *(pictured here), were popular with colonial theatergoers.*

the stage, and, following English custom, it was nearly always presented during the Christmas and Easter seasons for the edification of apprentices.

George Farquhar was the author of the two most popular comedies presented on the colonial stage, *The Recruiting Officer*, followed in popularity by *The Beaux' Stratagem*. The witty *Recruiting Officer* contains lines that border on the indecent, but the gaiety and rollicking good humor make partial amends for what may be lacking in propriety. Written in 1705, when all England was blazing with martial spirit and while the playwright himself was on a recruiting party, the play was in demand in America during those crises in which the colonies were threatened with involvement in the military activities of the Empire.

The Beggar's Opera was, by far, the most popular musical piece in a day when musicals were popular. Written by the genial humorist John Gay, this "Newgate Pastoral" was a long-time favorite with London audiences. Through the adventures of a highwayman, Captain Macheath, Gay satirized Italian opera, court modes, marriage customs of the aristocracy, and, especially, the political life of the age of Sir Robert Walpole. It is to be suspected, however, that colonial audiences overlooked the mordant satire and agreed with Dr. Johnson's evaluation, "There is in it so much of real London life, so much brilliant wit, and such a variety of airs, which, from early association of ideas engage, soothe, and enliven the mind, that no performance which the theatre exhibits delights me more.". . .

Almost every program of the colonial stage included a main attraction followed by an afterpiece. Afterpieces originally were used as "Crutches to our weakest Plays" and were not presented with the better pieces, as they would "dishonor our best Authors, in such bad company." Once introduced, however, their popularity was so great that they became a regular feature of each night's entertainment. Usually, they were farces, built around a singular situation or a case of mistaken identity, and sometimes musical productions of two or three acts. They were always light and designed to end the evening in a burst of gaiety. The favorite afterpiece in America, as in England, was the pantomime. Though not quite the same thing as *commedia dell'arte*, English pantomime, as developed by John Rich, combined the stock characters and situations of the harlequinade with elements from classic myths, folk tales, or contemporary events. They leaned heavily on scenic display, spectacle, dance, and acrobatics, and they were often cited as evidence of the low taste of audiences. The basic cast of the harlequinade included Harlequin, the lover of Columbine; Pantaloon, her father; and the Clown, the bumbling servant of Harlequin. Pantaloon constantly attempted to interfere with the courtship of Harlequin and Columbine, and out of this stock situation developed a flurry of tricks and feats of agility.

Among those fringe benefits to American culture offered by the colonial theater were musical interludes and similar entertainments that often set catchy lyrics to classical tunes (notably compositions of Arne and Handel), thereby subtly tuning the American ear to good music. Several actors who developed on the colonial stage were rated by competent critics as the equals of many favorites of the London theaters. The professional theater popularized the presentation of plays in schools and encouraged the art of public speaking, the latter flourishing to a remarkable degree in the revolutionary generation.

Contributions to American Culture and Art

The literary influence of the colonial theater cannot be measured, especially since it encouraged so few to turn to playwriting, but it has been claimed that two of the most famous utterances of the revolutionary era came from the story of *Cato*. Patrick Henry's defiant "Give me liberty or give me death," and Nathan Hale's pathetic "I regret that I have but one life to lose for my country," were echoes, it is said, of lines from that play.

"The Arts," Benjamin Franklin once wrote, "delight to travel westward. After the first cares for the necessities of life are over, we shall come to think of the embellishments." This observation, by a sage who was always wise beyond his years, sums up the importance of the colonial theater more succinctly than could any other statement. The players brought the dramatic arts westward, preparing the way for future embellishments in the shape of a native theater after the shackles of colonialism were broken. Yet, the colonial theater was an example of the pace and strength of colonial America, struggling against almost insurmountable odds and always growing stronger through experience.

Taverns of the South

Ivor Noël Hume

Chief archaeologist at colonial Williamsburg and writer Ivor Noël Hume explores the culture surrounding the popular taverns of the colonial era. Highly regarded in his field, Hume has written fifteen books on antiques and archaeology and was formerly the field archaeologist for London's Guildhall Museum. In the following selection, Hume describes the typical appearance of the establishments, their modes of serving and entertaining, the drinking preferences of the taverns' patrons, and the large role the tavern played in southern culture. Taverns gave both residents and visitors a place to conduct business, dine, drink, gamble, sleep, and socialize.

"After Dinner we came back to Williamsburg," wrote a French visitor in 1765. "Never was a more disagreable Place than this at Present. In the Day Time People hurying back and forwards from the Capitoll to the Taverns, and at Night, carousing and drinking in one Chamber and Box and Dice in another, which continues till Morning commonly, there is not a publick House in Virginia but have their Tables all batered with ye Boxes which shews the extravagant Disposition of the Planters."

A Center of Social Life

The taverns of Williamsburg, and the Raleigh in particular, were the temporary homes of the majority of visitors to the city at Public Times. They served as places of business and tended as well to the needs of those who came to eat, drink, or gamble away their money, their tobacco crop, and even the land on which they grew it. In short the taverns or "ordinaries" as they were more frequently termed, were centers of *life* in colonial Virginia. They existed in every town and village and were stationed along the roads for the benefit of travelers and their horses.

Some, like the Swan Tavern at Yorktown and the Raleigh in Williamsburg, were as well known in Virginia as were London's Boar's Head, Mermaid, or Rose taverns in England. Indeed, it has been claimed that the Raleigh on Duke of Gloucester Street in Williamsburg was the most famous tavern in the South, ranking alongside the noted City Tavern in Philadelphia or Fraunces' Tavern in New York. . . .

Appearance

Although the Swan was the most important of Yorktown's taverns, there are few clues to its original appearance. The best are to be found in the inventory of landlord James Mitchell who died in 1772 "in his sixty eighth year; a Man who was as generally esteemed as any in the Colony." From this inventory we learn that there were six beds in "the Rooms Upstairs," which suggest that lodging facilities were somewhat limited. Although we do not know the size of the beds, there is ample evidence from other sources to show that tavern visitors frequently shared beds at rates advertised as "for lodging in clean sheets, one in a bed, sixpence; if two in a bed, threepence and three farthings; if more than two, nothing."

The Swan's principal room on the first floor was furnished with twelve leather-bottomed chairs, and walnut and mahogany tables, one of these being "for Cards lined." Like most eighteenth century taverns of any standing the Swan had its billiard room, while the room next to it housed two pairs of backgammon tables and a chessboard with two sets of men. The room described as the "Chamber" was almost certainly the public eating and drinking room, for besides its tables and chairs it contained a goodly array of "blue and white china plates . . . red and white china plates" and a variety of bowls, teapots, tea cups, coffee cups, glass decanters and wine, cider, and punch glasses. . . .

An English visitor to Yorktown in 1736 noted that "The Taverns are many here, and much frequented," which was hardly surprising in a town that was a major port and a haven for carousing seamen. Fortunately for its more genteel inhabitants, the town lay on two levels: the stores, warehouses, and more disreputable places of relaxation close to the shore, and the better homes ranged along the bluff behind. . . .

Drinking and Service Habits

Although there were undoubtedly many drinking places and brothels on Virginia waterfronts that were disreputable enough to make a colonial dame swoon, the majority of taverns were as respectable as the trade permitted. Tables of rates and prices were set by the county courts and these were required to be displayed in the public rooms. In addition, the tavern keepers were required by statute to refrain from permitting on the Sabbath Day "any person to tipple and drink any more than is necessary," a pleasant regulation which, while mindful of the solemnities of Sunday, was equally cognizant of the colonists' need to quench their thirst on a hot summer day and to warm their vitals on a cold winter's night. An excellent idea of the range of the liquid fortification available in eighteenth century Yorktown or Williamsburg is to be found in the list of rates authorized by the York County Court in March 1709–10. In it we find that "Wine of Virginia Produce" was the most expensive you could buy, selling for five shillings a quart, while "Virginia Beer & Cyder" were the cheapest and were dispensed at threepence three farthings a quart. Among the imported lubricants were "Canary & Sherry . . . Red & White Lisbon . . . Western Islands Wines . . . French Brandy . . . French Brandy Punch or French Brandy Flip . . . Rum & Virginia Brandy . . . Rum Punch & Rum flip" and English beer. In the following year an addition to the list tabled "Roger's best Virg aile" at a rate of sixpence a quart, half the price of English beer and twopence farthing more expensive than the Virginia beer and cider. This entry would not be particularly noteworthy were it not for the fact that this is the earliest reference yet found to William Rogers, brewer of Yorktown and operator of an extremely important potting factory where he appropriately manufactured tavern mugs and jugs.

While wines and spirits were generally served in glasses, most taverns dispensed ale, beer, and cider in pewter or pottery mugs; of the latter the blue and gray stoneware tankards from the Rhineland were the most common with mugs of English brown stoneware in second place. The German tankards were made to hold standard quantities and marks of capacity were usually painted on the sides in cobalt. The English mugs, on the other hand, were not so marked, but they were made to rigid standards of capacity and were required to be impressed with an official stamp to distinguish them from those that did not contain accurate measures. The majority of the brown stoneware mugs were of half-pint capacity, but some were of massive proportions and held one or even two quarts. An inventory in the letters of William Beverly listing goods to be sent from England to Virginia in 1740 were "gallon Stone Juggs" and "pottle Stone muggs upright sides"—a pottle being two quarts. . . .

A Place of Historical Value

Unfortunately there is little documentary evidence to tell us of the activities and character of the taverns of seventeenth century Jamestown. In marked contrast are the hostelries of Williamsburg whose histories are well known, and any one of them could be used as a typical example of the eighteenth century. But as I have already intimated, the Raleigh was the most famous of them all, not because its liquor or its cuisine were particularly outstanding but because it held a status in the town that was virtually that of a public building. Legislators repaired there to continue their debates after leaving the Capitol, and when in May 1774, Governor Dunmore dissolved the House of Burgesses for objecting to the closing of the port of Boston after the tea party, eighty-nine of the members met in the Raleigh's "long room" to form an association to ban imports from Britain. In happier times the Governor's Council undertook its official entertaining at the Raleigh; the Phi Beta Kappa Society is believed to have been founded there in 1776; and two years later Governor Botetourt entertained there after the oath-taking ceremony at the Capitol. It was in the Apollo Room of the tavern that young Thomas Jefferson danced with his Belinda and afterward wrote to his friend John Page of Rosewell that "Last night, as merry as agreeable company and dancing with Belinda in the Apollo could make me, I never could have thought the succeeding Sun would have seen me so wretched. . . ."

Mingling with the echoes of the minuet and the bark of table-pounding politicians the psychic among us may hear the sounds of commerce, land sales being transacted, crops sold, and servants hired, while outside on the steps or porch everything from slaves to ships was sold by auction. . . .

Colonial Amusement and the Role of the Tavern

When we try to envisage the way in which the colonists entertained themselves and each other, archaeology tends to let us down. It is true that we can unearth occasional gaming pieces, simple children's toys, and huge quantities of broken wine bottles; yet somehow these things are no more evocative of excitement, laughter, and happiness than is morning sunlight falling on the full ash trays and empty glasses of last night's party; the magic has departed. Yet it lives on in the pages of history. From an announcement in the *Virginia Gazette* for December 7th, 1739, we can obtain a lively impression of the kind of "diversions" that passed the daylight hours in Williamsburg at Public Times:

> AND for the Entertainment and Diversion of all Gentlemen and others, that shall resort thereto, the following PRIZES are given to be contended for, at the Fair, *viz.*
>
> A good Hat to be cudgell'd for: and to be given to the Person that fairly wins it, by the common Rules of Play.
>
> A Saddle of 40s. Value, to be run for, once round the Mile Course, adjacent to this City, by any Horse, Mare or Gelding, carrying Horseman's Weight, and allowing Weight for Inches. A handsome Bridle to be given to the Horse that comes in second. And a good Whip to the Horse that comes in third.
>
> A Pair of Silver Buckles, Value 20s. to be run for by Men, from the College to the Capitol. A Pair of Shoes to be given to him that comes in second. And a Pair of Gloves to the third.
>
> A Pair of Pumps to be danc'd for by Men.
>
> A Handsome Firelock to be exercis'd for; and given to the Person that performs the Manual Exercise best.
>
> A Pig, with his Tail soap'd, to be run after; and to be given to the Person that catches him, and lifts him off the Ground fairly by the Tail.

To the modern [world] these may seem but simple rustic amusements; yet in their proper setting of cheering, wagering spectators, contestants competing steamy-breathed in the brisk winter air, and tavern keepers ready with hot drinks and good food, such honest pleasures had much to commend them.

Puritan Views of Revelry and Bodily Pleasure

William Bradford

Author William Bradford was the governor of Plymouth Plantation, the community of Puritans who arrived in the New World on the *Mayflower*. For over thirty years, Bradford oversaw this early American community, and he recorded one of the earliest histories of New England in his book *Of Plymouth Plantation*, from which the following selection is excerpted. In retelling the trials and tribulations of the Pilgrims, Bradford provides useful firsthand insights into the quality of life and character of the people of this area and also inadvertently accentuates their prejudices. The writer intends for his work to both provide a history of the settlement and promote Puritan ideals to future and contemporary readers. In this selection, Bradford expresses his moral indignation toward a man named Thomas Morton, who he contends encourages people to act in ways unbecoming of a devout Puritan. Bradford's prose reflects both his religiosity and his fear of anyone who has a differing worldview.

There came over one Captain Wollaston (a man of pretty parts) and with him three or four more of some eminency, who brought with them a great many servants, with provisions and other implements for to begin a plantation. And pitched themselves in a place within the Massachusetts which they called after their Captain's name, Mount Wollaston. Amongst whom was one Mr. Morton, who it should seem had some small adventure of his own or other men's amongst them, but had little respect amongst them, and was slighted by the meanest servants. Having continued there some time, and not finding things to answer their expectations nor profit to arise as they looked for, Cap-

---

William Bradford, *Of Plymouth Plantation, 1620–1647*. New York: Knopf, 1966.

tain Wollaston takes a great part of the servants and transports them to Virginia, where he puts them off at good rates, selling their time to other men; and writes back to one Mr. Rasdall (one of his chief partners and accounted their merchant) to bring another part of them to Virginia likewise, intending to put them off there as he had done the rest. And he, with the consent of the said Rasdall, appointed one Fitcher to be his Lieutenant and govern the remains of the Plantation till he or Rasdall returned to take further order thereabout.

Through Words, Food, and Drink, Morton Changes the Servants' Minds

But this Morton abovesaid, having more craft than honesty (who had been a kind of pettifogger of Furnival's Inn) in the others' absence watches an opportunity (commons being but hard amongst them) and got some strong drink and other junkets and made them a feast; and after they were merry, he began to tell them he would give them good counsel. "You see," saith he, "that many of your fellows are carried to Virginia, and if you stay till this Rasdall return, you will also be carried away and sold for slaves with the rest. Therefore I would advise you to thrust out this Lieutenant Fitcher, and I, having a part in the Plantation, will receive you as my partners and consociates; so may you be free from service, and we will converse, plant, trade, and live together as equals and support and protect one another," or to like effect. This counsel was easily received, so they took opportunity and thrust Lieutenant Fitcher out o' doors, and would suffer him to come no more amongst them, but forced him to seek bread to eat and other relief from his neighbours till he could get passage for England.

Morton and His Followers Lead a Life Contrary to Puritan Values

After this they fell to great licentiousness and led a dissolute life, pouring out themselves into all profaneness. And Morton became Lord of Misrule, and maintained (as it were) a School of Atheism. And after they had got some goods into their hands, and got much by trading with the Indians, they spent it as vainly in quaffing and drinking, both wine and strong waters in great excess (and, as some reported) £10 worth in a morning. They also set up a maypole, drinking and dancing about it many days together, inviting the Indian women for their consorts, dancing and frisking together like so many fairies, or furies, rather; and worse practices. As if they had anew revived and celebrated the feasts of the Roman goddess Flora, or the beastly practices of the mad Bacchanalians. Morton likewise, to show his poetry composed sundry rhymes and verses, some tending to lasciviousness, and others to the detraction and scandal of some persons, which he affixed to this idle or idol maypole. They changed also the name of their place, and instead of calling it Mount Wollaston they call it Merry-mount, as if this jollity would have lasted ever. But this continued not long, for after Morton was sent for England (as follows to be declared) shortly after came over that worthy gentleman Mr. John Endecott, who brought over a patent under the broad seal for the government of the Massachusetts. Who, visiting those parts, caused that maypole to be cut down and rebuked them for their profaneness and admonished them to look there should be better walking. So they or others now changed the name of their place again and called it Mount Dagon.

Trading and Befriending the Indians: Another Evil

Now to maintain this riotous prodigality and profuse excess, Morton, thinking himself lawless, and hearing what gain the French and fishermen made by trading of pieces, powder and shot to the Indians, he as the head of this consortship began the practice of the same in these parts. And first he taught them how to use them, to charge and discharge, and what proportion of powder to give the piece, according to the size or bigness of the same; and what shot to use for fowl and what for deer. And having thus instructed them, he employed some of them to hunt and fowl for him, so as they became far more active in that employment than any of the English, by reason of their swiftness of foot and nimbleness of body, being also quick-sighted and by continual exercise well knowing the haunts of all sorts of game. So as when they saw the execution that a piece would do, and the benefit that might come by the same, they became mad (as it were) after them and would not stick to give any price they could attain to for them; accounting their bows and arrows but baubles in comparison of them.

And here I may take occasion to bewail the mischief that this wicked man began in these parts, and which since, base covetousness prevailing in men that should know better, has now at length got the upper hand and made this thing common, notwithstanding any laws to the contrary. So as the Indians are full of pieces all over, both fowling pieces, muskets, pistols, etc. They have also their moulds to make shot of all sorts, as musket bullets, pistol bullets, swan and goose shot, and of smaller sorts. Yea some have seen them have their screw-plates to make screw-pins themselves when they want them, with sundry other implements, wherewith they are ordinarily better fitted and furnished than the English themselves. Yea, it is well known that they will have powder and shot when the English want it nor cannot get it; and that in a time of war or danger, as experience hath manifested, that when lead hath been scarce and men for their own defense would gladly have given a groat a pound, which is dear enough, yet hath it been bought up and sent to other places and sold to such as trade it with the Indians at 12*d* the pound. And it is like they give 3*s* or 4*s* the pound, for they will have it at any rate. And these things have been done in the same times when some of their neighbours and friends are daily killed by the Indians, or are in danger thereof and live but at the Indians' mercy. Yea some, as they have acquainted them with all other things, have told them how gunpowder is made, and all the materials in it, and that they are to be had in their own land; and I am confident, could they attain to make saltpeter, they would teach them to make powder.

O, the horribleness of this villainy! How many both Dutch and English have been lately slain by those Indians thus furnished, and no remedy provided; nay, the evil more increased, and the blood of their brethren sold for gain (as is to be feared) and in what danger all these colonies are in is too well known. O that princes and parliaments would take some timely order to prevent this mischief and at length to suppress it by some exemplary punishment upon some of these gain-thirsty murderers, for they deserve no better title, before their colonies in these parts be overthrown by these barbarous savages thus armed with their own weapons, by these evil instruments and traitors to their neighbours and country. . . .

Because of His Behavior, the Immoderate Morton Is Arrested, Only to Return Again

Morton they brought away to Plymouth, where he was kept till a ship went from the Isle of Shoals for England, with which he was sent to the Council of New England, and letters written to give them information of his course and carriage. And also one was sent at their common charge to inform their Honours more particularly and to prosecute against him. But he fooled of the messenger, after he was gone from hence, and though he went for England yet nothing was done to him, not so much as rebuked, for aught was heard, but returned the next year. Some of the worst of the company were dispersed and some of the more modest kept the house till he should be heard from. But I have been too long about so unworthy a person, and bad a cause.

Chronology

1492

Christopher Columbus reaches the Americas, claims them for Spain, and initiates centuries of exploration, conquest, and colonization of the continent.

1585

The first English colony is established at Roanoke Island, North Carolina. The colony later vanishes without a trace.

1607

The colony of Jamestown is started in Virginia. The first permanent colony in America, Jamestown was named after King James of England.

1619

The first African slaves arrive at Jamestown, Virginia.

1620

Puritan Pilgrims arriving on the *Mayflower* found Plymouth colony in Massachusetts.

1626

Peter Minuit of the Dutch West India Company purchases the island of Mahattan for twenty-nine dollars' worth of cloth, beads, trinkets, and tools.

1630

The Puritans establish nearly a dozen towns in Massachusetts, including Boston.

1636

Harvard College is founded by Massachusetts Bay Colony to both teach the ministerial profession and to provide instruction in the arts and sciences.

1648

By law, rebellious children over sixteen years of age in Massachusetts can be executed for striking their parents.

1656

The first Quaker populations arrive in the New World. The first public collection of books is set up in Boston. This library was originally a private collection given to the city at the death of the books' owner, Robert Keayne.

1673

A regular mail circuit is established between New York and Boston. In summer, the trip takes one week; in winter, it is a two-week journey.

1681

William Penn begins to establish the colony of Pennsylvania, which literally means "Penn's Woods."

1690

The first paper mill is set up in Germantown, Pennsylvania. Massachusetts issues the first paper money in the American colonies.

1692

The Salem Witch Crisis occurs, as young Puritan girls falsely accuse other villagers of witchcraft, thus initiating a paranoid religious frenzy in which many townspeople are unfairly imprisoned and executed.

1704

The first weekly newspaper, the *Boston News-Letter*, is founded.

1712

Slaves rebel in New York City. The first public coach for hire appears outside a Boston tavern.

1716

Despite moral and religious opposition, the first theater in the American colonies opens in Williamsburg, Virginia. The first lighthouse in the American colonies, the Boston Light, is constructed.

1720

Black slaves comprise a majority of the population in South Carolina.

1727

Benjamin Franklin forms the Junto Club (later to be renamed the American Philosophical Society) in Philadelphia, attesting to the area's interest and influence in the scientific and intellectual progress of American life.

1739

The Stono Rebellion in South Carolina marks one of the most infamous and bloody slave uprisings in colonial North America.

1755

Paper money is issued in Virginia.

1772

A regular stagecoach service between Boston and New York is established. The trip takes ten days to complete.

1776

American independence from colonial British rule is declared on July 2.

For Further Research

William Apess, *On Our Own Ground: The Complete Writings of William Apess, a Pequot.* Amherst: University of Massachusetts Press, 1992.

William Bartram, *The Travels of William Bartram.* New York: Dover, 1955.

Linda Baumgarten, *What Clothes Reveal: The Language of Clothing in Colonial and Federal America.* Williamsburg, VA: New Haven, 2002.

Lerone Bennett Jr., *The Shaping of Black America.* Chicago: Johnson, 1975.

Louise A. Breen, *Transgressing the Bounds: Subversive Enterprises Among the Puritan Elite in Massachusetts, 1630–1692.* New York: Oxford University Press, 2001.

Jon Butler, *Becoming America: The Revolution Before 1776.* Cambridge, MA: Harvard University Press, 2000.

Jane Carson, *Colonial Virginians at Play.* Williamsburg, VA: Colonial Williamsburg Foundation, 1989.

Susan Castillo and Ivy Schweitzer, eds., *The Literature of Colonial America: An Anthology.* Malden, MA: Blackwell, 2001.

John Demos, *A Little Commonwealth: Family Life in Plymouth Colony.* Oxford, UK: Oxford University Press, 1970.

Jonathan Edwards, *Puritan Sage: Collected Writings of Jonathan Edwards.* New York: Library, 1953.

Shirley Glubok, ed., *Home and Child Life in Colonial Days.* New York: Macmillan, 1969.

Larry Gragg, *The Salem Witch Crisis.* New York: Praeger, 1992.

David Freeman Hawke, *Everyday Life in Early America.* New York: Harper and Row, 1988.

Nathaniel Hawthorne, *The Scarlet Letter.* London: Penguin, 1999.

———, *Young Goodman Brown and Other Tales.* Oxford, UK: Oxford University Press, 1987.

Patricia Hermes, *The Starving Time.* New York: Scholastic, 2001.

Faith Jaycox, *The Colonial Era: An Eyewitness History.* New York: Facts On File, 2002.

Allan Keller, *Colonial America: A Compact History.* Wheeling, IL: Hawthorne, 1971.

James D. Kornwolf, *Architecture and Town Planning in Colonial North America.* Baltimore: Johns Hopkins University Press, 2002.

Karen Ordahl Kupperman, *Indians and English: Facing Off in Early America.* Ithaca, NY: Cornell University Press, 2000.

Almon Lauber, *Indian Slavery in Colonial Times.* Williamstown, MA: Corner House, 1970.

Charles H. Lincoln, ed., *Narratives of the Indian Wars.* New York: Barnes and Noble, 1966.

Arnold Madison, *How the Colonists Lived.* New York: McKay, 1981.

Gloria L. Main, *Peoples of a Spacious Land: Families and Cultures in Colonial New England.* Cambridge, MA: Harvard University Press, 2001.

Cotton Mather, *Cotton Mather on Witchcraft.* New York: Bell, 1974.

B. Edward McClellan, *Moral Education in America: Schools and the Shaping of Character from Colonial Times to the Present.* New York: Teachers College Press, 1999.

Kenneth Morgan, *Slavery and Servitude in Colonial North America.* Washington Square: New York University Press, 2001.

Mark A. Noll, *America's God: From Jonathan Edwards to Abraham Lincoln.* New York: Oxford University Press, 2002.

Jean M. O'Brien, *Dispossession by Degrees: Indian Land and Identity in Natick, Massachusetts, 1650–1790.* New York: Cambridge University Press, 1997.

Charles Orr, ed., *History of the Pequot War.* New York: AMS, 1980.

Thomas L. Purvis, *Colonial America to 1763.* New York: Facts On File, 1999.

Daniel K. Richter, *Facing East from Indian Country: A Native History of Early America.* Cambridge, MA: Harvard University Press, 2001.

Robert Blair Saint George, ed., *Possible Pasts: Becoming Colonial in Early America.* Ithaca, NY: Cornell University Press, 2000.

Thomas Scanlan, *Colonial Writing and the New World, 1583–1671: Allegories of Desire*. New York: Cambridge University Press, 1999.

Richard Slotkin and James Folsom, eds., *So Dreadfull a Judgment: Puritan Responses to King Philip's War, 1676–1677*. Middletown, CT: Wesleyan University Press, 1978.

Alden Vaughan, *New England Frontier: Puritans and Indians, 1620–1675*. New York: Norton, 1979.

Alden Vaughan and Edward W. Clark, eds., *Puritans Among the Indians: Accounts of Captivity and Redemption, 1676–1724*. Cambridge, MA: Harvard University Press, 1981.

Daniel Vickers, ed., *A Companion to Colonial America*. Malden, MA: Blackwell, 2003.

James M. Volo and Dorothy Denneen Volo, *Daily Life on the Old Colonial Frontier*. Westport, CT: Greenwood, 2002.

Thomas J. Wertenbaker, *The Age of Colonial Culture*. New York: New York University Press, 1949.

Phillis Wheatley, *The Collected Work of Phillis Wheatley*. New York: Oxford University Press, 1988.

Peter H. Wood, *Strange New Land: Africans in Colonial America, 1526–1776*. Oxford: Oxford University Press, 2003.

Louis B. Wright, *History of the Thirteen Colonies*. New York: American Heritage, 1967.

Feeny Ziner, *The Pilgrims and Plymouth Colony*. New York: American Heritage, 1966.

Index